"Joe Vitale is a true marketing, sales, and promotion genius."

—Dan Kennedy,
in his book *No B.S. Marketing to the Affluent*

"Just when you think you understand how the world works Joe Vitale comes along and takes you to a whole new place. He's engaging, entertaining, enlightening and—oh boy—does he ever stretch your thinking."

—Ian Percy,
Reg. Psych. and member
of both the U.S. and
Canadian Speaker Halls of Fame

"No one else I know of could help someone come up with a Barnum-like Big Idea and then help them take it to fruition, becoming a huge phenomenon, which means *big* money, fame, recognition, and unique world positioning. See Joe Vitale's outrageous list of accomplishments to know this is the real deal."

—David Garfinkel,
copywriter, author, consultant

The
Awakened
Millionaire

The Awakened Millionaire

A MANIFESTO FOR THE SPIRITUAL WEALTH MOVEMENT

Joe Vitale

WILEY

Cover image:
Cover design:

This book is printed on acid-free paper.

Copyright © 2016 by Hypnotic Marketing, Inc. All rights reserved

Published by John Wiley & Sons, Inc., Hoboken, New Jersey

Published simultaneously in Canada

For general information about our other products and services, please contact our Customer Care Department within the United States at (800) 762-2974, outside the United States at (317) 572-3993 or fax (317) 572-4002.

Wiley publishes in a variety of print and electronic formats and by print-on-demand. Some material included with standard print versions of this book may not be included in e-books or in print-on-demand. If this book refers to media such as a CD or DVD that is not included in the version you purchased, you may download this material at http://booksupport.wiley.com. For more information about Wiley products, visit www.wiley.com.

Library of Congress Cataloging-in-Publication Data:

Names: Vitale, Joe, 1953- author.
Title: The awakened millionaire : a manifesto for the spiritual wealth movement / Joe Vitale.
Description: Hoboken, New Jersey : John Wiley & Sons, 2016. | Includes
   bibliographical references and index.
Identifiers: LCCN 2016001658| ISBN 9781119264163 (cloth) | ISBN 9781119264187 (epub) |
ISBN 9781119264170 (epdf)
Subjects: LCSH: Wealth—Religious aspects. | Well-being—Religious aspects. |
   Success–Religious aspects.
Classification: LCC BL65.W42 V58 2016 | DDC 650.1—dc23 LC record available at
   http://lccn.loc.gov/2016001658

Printed in the United States of America

10 9 8 7 6 5 4 3 2 1

To you, the Awakened Millionaire

Fortune sides with him who dares.
                                    —Virgil

CONTENTS

PROMISE YOURSELF

To be so strong that nothing can disturb your peace of mind.

To talk health, happiness, and prosperity to every person you meet.

To make all your friends feel that there is something worthwhile in them.

To look at the sunny side of everything and make your optimism come true.

To think only of the best, to work only for the best, and to expect only the best.

To be just as enthusiastic about the success of others as you are about your own.

To forget the mistakes of the past and press on to the greater achievements of the future.

To wear a cheerful expression at all times and give a smile to every living creature you meet.

To give so much time to improving yourself that you have no time to criticize others.

To be too large for worry, too noble for anger, too strong for fear, and too happy to permit the presence of trouble.

To think well of yourself and to proclaim this fact to the world, not in loud word, but in great deeds.

To live in the faith that the whole world is on your side, so long as you are true to the best that is in you.

—The original *Optimist Creed*, written by Christian D. Larson
in his 1912 book, *Your Forces and How to Use Them*

THE AWAKENED MILLIONAIRE CREED

Awakened Millionaires are driven first by their passion, purpose, and mission.

The Awakened Millionaire uses money as a soulful tool to make a positive impact.

The Awakened Millionaire is persistently empowered, believing in themselves absolutely.

The Awakened Millionaire is committed to grow, improve, reinvent, and always discover.

The Awakened Millionaire is unshakably bold, takes risks, and does not hesitate.

The Awakened Millionaire is guided by the soulful resonance of their intuition.

The Awakened Millionaire knows wealth is everything they have, not just money.

The Awakened Millionaire holds a deep gratitude for all they have and achieve.

The Awakened Millionaire is permanently connected to Universal abundance.

The Awakened Millionaire is generous, ethical, and focuses on the good of others.

The Awakened Millionaire champions the win–win–win.

The Awakened Millionaire soulfully shares their entrepreneurial gifts.

The Awakened Millionaire leads by example as the catalyst for transformation in others.

WHATEVER may be said in praise of poverty, the fact remains that it is not possible to live a really complete or successful life unless one is rich. No man can rise to his greatest possible height in talent or soul development unless he has plenty of money; for to unfold the soul and to develop talent he must have many things to use, and he cannot have these things unless he has money to buy them with.

—Wallace Wattles, *The Science of Getting Rich*

FOREWORD

This is my opus. This manifesto is 30 years in the making. I've never felt more convinced about anything I've taught or shared before.

The Awakened Millionaire movement isn't just to build your future, rising up and succeeding both financially and spiritually. This is about all of our futures. What you can become as an Awakened Millionaire is beyond your own profound success. It's about what you can give back to the world, to a world that needs it. It's about you becoming a force for good, for change. It's about you making a difference. And to do that, you must succeed both financially and spiritually. That's how you will become the powerhouse that is an Awakened Millionaire. You must thrive, for all our sakes.

The world needs you to succeed.

The vision is far-reaching, the call to action is strong, and the stakes are high. So I want to make it crystal clear why you should listen to me— for every success I've had, every challenge I've overcome, and every dream I've achieved has led me to this moment, here, with you.

I wasn't born with a silver spoon in my mouth. In fact, during my time living on the streets of Dallas, Texas, a silver spoon would've been my salvation. Instead, I lived in poverty for 10 years. Every challenge to your own success I've likely experienced. And in the depths of my poverty, the challenges we all face are amplified to a deafening level.

Today, I've built a lifestyle that transcends what my homeless self would've considered possible. I am a multimillionaire blessed with the level of wealth and freedom I want for you. But I'm also deep on my own spiritual path, devoted to growing more, experiencing more, and awakening more. It is a life-long journey. I love every moment.

It's taken decades to get to where I am today. And I'm genuinely proud of the accomplishments I've achieved. I'm sharing these not to brag, but simply to prove that I walk what I talk and I live what I teach.

Whether it's flying out to Kuwait as a guest of a princess, paid six figures to speak at her event, or whether it's the son of the man who produced the Beatles wanting me in a movie and television show he's producing . . .

Whether it's the almost 50 books I've written, including international best-sellers such as *The Attractor Factor* or *The Secret Prayer* . . . or it's the record-breaking self-help programs sold by publishers like the famous Nightingale-Conant . . .

Whether it's pioneering Internet marketing, writing one of the first books ever published about it, using the Internet to outsell a Harry Potter book . . . or selling a high-ticket training program making half a million dollars in three days . . .

Whether it's traveling around the world, speaking in countries as diverse as Russia, Peru, or Poland . . . Or being a keynote speaker at major events in the United States for the National Speakers Associations and megawealth events with Donald Trump and Tony Robbins on the same bill . . .

Whether it's inventing *Hypnotic Writing*, *Hypnotic Marketing*, *Buying Trances*, The Secret Mirror, The Secret Reflection, Miracles Coaching®, Wealth Trigger, Hyper-Wealth, and much more . . . or simply knowing how to generate ideas, package them, and market them to the masses . . .

Whether it's attracting national media exposure being on everything from *Larry King Live* (twice) to Donny Deutsch's *Big Idea* TV show, to being on ABC, Fox, CNN, CNBC, and more . . . or being in 15 movies, with *The Secret* being the most famous . . .

Whether it's bringing the spiritual healing system called *ho'oponopono* to the world, through my books *Zero Limits* and *AT Zero*, reaching an estimated 5 million people . . . or following the spiritual urge near the age of 60 to myself as a musician recording 15 albums at last count . . .

Whether it's developing a spiritual approach to wealth, ignoring cutthroat methods and always focusing on a balanced, healthy approach to success, based on passion and purpose . . . or knowing how to create win–win–win negotiations and conduct business from the heart . . .

Whether it's listening to virtually anyone for about 20 minutes and seeing or creating a unique money-making idea specific to them . . . or creating *Operation YES*, a movement to end homelessness, raising funds for those in poverty, or teaching those who struggle with homelessness to think big, confront limitations, and go for their highest ideals . . .

Whether it's discovering a "missing secret" in self-development, the idea of *counterintentions* and teaching others how anyone can overcome and accelerate their results . . . or becoming an expert on the Law of Attraction, knowing how to use it, teach it, and go beyond it. . . .

I have achieved financial success. I have tasted spiritual awakening. And I've taught millions of people the path to get there. This is the next level.

These successes have become my legacy. But I tell you them to earn your trust, as the path ahead will require it.

I have something to teach you. I want to inspire you to go for and achieve your dreams. And I want you to do it by following your passion. When you learn how to turn your passion into profit, and to make a difference in the world by expressing the uniqueness that is you, your life will become miraculous. You will have discovered Spiritual Wealth.

And, at that point, you will become an Awakened Millionaire.

This manifesto is my tool to accomplish that noble dream for you.

As you'll see, the book itself is slightly unorthodox. But it serves a specific strategy: to awaken your logical and emotional selves, two sides that must unite as you start your path to becoming an Awakened Millionaire.

This manifesto is a rallying cry for you to join a movement.

Please read it, absorb it, reflect on it, and put it into action.

I'm on a mission to help elevate the world from the needless struggles we face. It begins by helping you transform and achieve the financial and spiritual dreams you hold.

This is for you. This is for us.

Will you join me?

Joe Vitale
Austin, Texas
www.awakenedmillionaireacademy.com/begin

INTRODUCTION

Vishen Lakhiani

I've been a Joe Vitale fan for as long as I can remember. I first discovered Joe's books when I was a college student at the University of Michigan and his books opened my eyes to the idea that I didn't have to go through the traditional path: get good grades, graduate, find a 9-to-5 job, earn a living. Rather, his books opened me up to the idea that there was more to life than just this path that everyone else goes on. This is why I'm honored to be writing this preface.

Joe's particular book *The Awakened Millionaire* serves an important purpose because it's a manifesto for the globe. It's about profiting; it's a wake up call to save people from going down a traditional path in life that is the path of working hard to get a job, to slave away from 9:00 to 5:00, to get some money so you can pay the bills, so you can survive. Most people are in survival mode when what we should be is in thriving mode. So this book could very well save you and shift you to a path where you are actually living a life of meaning.

See, the problem with the education system is that we ask people, "What do you want to be when you grown up?" And the nature of that question, and the nature of the idea itself, suggests that we grow up to take on a particular career, to earn money, to pay the bills, to survive.

But a better question might be, "What do you really enjoy doing that you might be able to turn into a gift for the world?" This is the question that this book has you answer. It's about spiritual wealth. It's about making peace with money. Not seeing money as something you have to slog to earn, but money as a reward for you doing good deeds for the world and fulfilling your mission.

And there's something amazing that happens when you work on something that you feel is a mission. It drives you. It inspires you. It motivates you. Life doesn't feel like an uphill climb. It almost feels as if you have the wind behind your back as you move towards this mission. When you do this, work dissolves. Work ceases to exist in your vocabulary because when you're working on your mission, nothing makes you happier. The money is just a beautiful side effect.

This book is the best of Joe's work so far—perhaps his greatest work out of 30 years and 50 books. It is designed to inspire people to stretch, to grow, to serve, to awaken. The first part of the book talks from a "we perspective" to help you realize that we are all one and because we are all one, what could be more important than creating a mission that serves a collective humanity?

The second part of the book is about you . . . it's from a "you perspective" to address your own personal call to action. It helps you identify your mission, how to make sure the mission is right, how to monetize your mission.

Just as few books in history have actually changed the course of history, this book, the manifesto, is designed to do the same for a new generation. Your generation. My generation. The time is now. The book is here.

Thank you.

Vishen Lakhiani
Founder, Mindvalley
Author, *Code of the Extraordinary Mind*

ACKNOWLEDGMENTS

W here do I begin? I have many people to thank. Without Mitch Van Dusen's enthusiasm, persistence, dedication, and passion, this book may have remained an idea that never hatched into being. He and his wife, Paloma Mele, were directly responsible for creating the foundation for this manifesto. Matt Holt and my friends at John Wiley & Sons, Elizabeth Gildea and Shannon Vargo, saw the value of this book and quickly offered to publish it. Dawn Kilgore at Wiley provided excellent editorial feedback. The Statbrook Group, consisting of Frank Mangano, Steve G. Jones, Paul Mascetta, and Glenn Cucurullo, always support my product ideas; together we have created an online product and a movement around this book at www.awakenedmillionaireacademy. com/begin. Suzanne Burns and Zion Chatelle have been with me a long time, as friends and assistants, without whom few of my projects would get done. Achieve Today, who run my Miracles Coaching® program, are all beautiful souls who help carry my work into the world. And of course, Nerissa, my love, is always there for me. I love you all and thank you all.

PROLOGUE

A bizarre, schizophrenic battle is raging in your head. You are at the front lines, a gun in your blister-stained hands, as you fire fanatically and continuously into a blinding haze of fog.

You cannot see beyond it.

But the enemy is there, menacing, a rabid dog. Occasionally you see a shadow shimmering through the haze —a flash of movement without a shape to define it. You want to say you see faces, bodies, and trees, but nothing is clear except the battle. The battle is a behemoth impossible to miss. The enemy must be a behemoth as well.

But all you really know of the enemy is the fog that hides it. The fog that never flees. It is as persistent as you are.

To your left and right, you see long lines of others, men and women, engaged with the same compulsion and vigor. Some yell ferociously, spraying waves of bullets into the fog. Some simply keep firing on, stoically committed.

No one looks like a hardened soldier or a trained fighter. You are all just people. Everyone looks hardened by exhaustion.

You are tired, your bones weary and your soul sagging. Callouses stain your hands. Dirt has woven itself into the threads of your clothes. Your shoulders are tense and contorted, the look of someone permanently embracing a rifle.

Still, no one dares rest. The enemy is there. The war is real. The stakes are desperately high. That's all you must know.

You don't remember when this war started.

You don't remember the face of the enemy you fight.

You don't remember the last time you laid down.

Doubts have tugged at you, but your soulful conviction has never left you.

You do not indulge the doubts. You are fighting for good. You are fighting for what's right. You are fighting for your own survival.

That's all you must remember, so you never let it go.

You must stay true and press on. So you do.

You pause a moment and rest your eyes. And then you feel the warm hand rest on your shoulder.

You would've startled with shot nerves, but the soft touch is kind and disarming.

"Come with me. You must see something." The woman's voice is soft.

She is dressed in plain clothes. No fatigues. No weapons. But you see the old callouses on her trigger hand. They are not like yours. They've softened.

There is something quietly compelling about her. She seems . . . good. A good person. Calm and collected. Her posture is sure, yet soft.

Why is she here?

You shake your head. You cannot abandon the cause. You cannot retreat from your post.

Yet you stand.

You lay your weapon down, step away from your bunker, and quietly follow. Your fellow fighters turn and stare with venom in their eyes.

Your body is still buzzing from the vibrations of your gun, your arms uncomfortable and awkward with no weapon to hold.

Guilt and rage flash to your face as the blood drains to your feet.

You feel traitorous and treacherous.

But she walks, and you follow.

Muscle spasms and weak knees . . . you are uncomfortable. You don't remember how long it's been since you've walked.

But she keeps walking, and you keep following.

As you walk by your fellow soldiers hard at war, you see a futility you've never acknowledged before.

We are not soldiers, you say to yourself. We are not soldiers.

You've lost yourself in your head before you realize you've reached the end of the ranks. Your guide has climbed up and out of the trench, and begun walking, without fear. . . .

Why are we going towards the enemy lines?

Your pains and curiosities are replaced by dread and confusion. But you don't stop.

The fear rushes blood into your cheeks. You feel lightheaded. But you say nothing. You are petrified. But you keep walking.

Where is she taking you?

And then she stops. She points to a small hill to your right and gestures to it with an open hand.

You quietly climb the hill ahead of her. She walks beside you, comfortably walking at your strained pace. It feels kind and compassionate.

At the summit you turn around.

There it is. The battlefield. As you'd never imagined.

On the left, you see the sparkling light of muzzle flashes shrouded in fog, the guns of your fellow soldiers cracking with furious desperation.

On the right, you finally see beyond the fog.

There's nothing there.

No enemies, no gargantuan war machines, no frightful beasts.

Only a small forest of trees riddled with aimless bullets.

The involuntary gasp that escapes surprises you nearly as much as the site in front of you.

Every muscle in your body rattles with horror.

Your wide eyes pressed urgently against their sockets.

There is nothing there!

You grab her hand out of quick impulse and squeeze with ferocious confusion.

You mean to scream it out, but all that emerges is a strained whisper, "What have we been fighting for?"

She turns her head to you, with kindness in her eyes.

"For the love of money."

SECTION ONE

We

CHAPTER 1

The Truth

Money is not required to buy one necessity of the soul.
　　　　　　　　　　　　　　　　　—Henry David Thoreau

True or false:

Money is the root of all evil.
Money is the great destroyer.
Money can't buy happiness.
Money can't buy peace of mind.
Money corrupts absolutely.
Money hardens the heart.
Money is our madness.
Money is our prison.
Money controls us.
Money changes us.
Money makes us greedy.
Money makes us poor.

We are at war with money. We don't know when it started, or even why. But it feels right. It is the right war to wage, because we are more important than money. Our souls are in danger. Money should have no power over us. But it does. So we sing the battle cry.

We curse it. We curse it with pleasure, with anger, with spite, with venom.

Our souls rail against it as if it is all that's rotten with humanity.

We hate the wicked control it commands over us.

We resent its spiteful disregard for the stress it breeds.

We scorn the greed it births.

We brood over the sly way it eats away at our health, our longevity, and our happiness.

We spite it for making us helpless victims to its power.

We whine like spoiled children for its gift of misery.

We would burn it gleefully, bill by bill, if we didn't love it so much.

Yes, we are in love with money.

Whatever this fabricated war might be, it can't touch this insatiable desire to have it, hold it, covet it and cherish it.

We dream of bulging pockets and oversized paychecks.

We lust for this magical money freedom.

We revere it with blatant disregard for the consequences.

We're convinced we need it to buy our happiness.

We're jealous of those that have it.

We moan when we lose it.

We rejoice when we gain it.

We beg for it, plead for it, fight for it, cry for it.

We would violently curse a man who gleefully burned it, bill by bill.

What madness! What a twisted way to move through life!

If we had the same kind of relationship with our lovers, it would be dysfunctional and emotionally abusive. *I love you, I need you, I want more of you. You disgust me, you poison me. You're mine, all mine. You love everybody else, but not me.*

We are in a relationship with money whether we like it. It's not going away. It will not die. We live with money and money lives with us. Yet we fight, and fight, and fight. Struggle, struggle, and struggle.

This vicious cycle seems to be our fate.

And yet, as we fight, struggle, love, and hate, there is a small group of people who have it, hold it, and don't need it. People soaked in prosperity, having everything they could want. Everything, including mission and purpose. People who taste profound success while money is the least of their passions.

They neither love it, nor hate it.

They neither struggle with it, nor fight it.

They command it, yet respect it.

They don't fight for it, but they give with it.

And somehow they keep making money.

But this enlightened approach is far from the norm. And we have no help from the world around us to gain this enlightenment, much less even recognize the potential for enlightenment. Let us see how the mental poison keeps away the enlightenment.

A man drives down Route 180 in St. Louis, Missouri on his way to work, when his 1993 Toyota Corolla suddenly begins belching smoke and vapor from under the hood. He doesn't have the money to pay for repairs, but if he can't make it to work, he won't get paid his hourly wage. Not having a credit card, or any other recourse, he quickly trots to the closest storefront that promises payday loans. In hours, he has a $500 loan, and gets his Corolla to a repair shop. Two weeks later, he gets his paycheck, but he can't quite pull the cash together to pay back the short-term loan. The debt turns into $644 in one day, and grows staggeringly over the course of the next few months. The payday loan company finally sues him, and he loses everything he has, including his job.

He concludes, *Money is evil.*

Two sisters convene at a lawyer's office to hear their mother's last will and testament for the first time. They learn that the elder sister has been left the majority of their mother's estate, and the younger sister has been left a smaller amount locked in a trust. Later, in the older sister's living room, the younger one angrily asks why she has been so poorly rewarded in the will. The older sister cautiously comments on the younger's problems with drugs and alcohol, as well as her absence at the hospital for the last few months. The younger sister flies into a rage, and so begins a fight so awful they cannot speak to one another. Even after they reconnect years later, the younger sister feels resentment. The older one forever feels guilt over keeping her full share, yet never offers her sister any financial assistance for fear of insulting her.

They conclude, *Money is the great destroyer.*

Every day for 23 years, a man starts his day at his local deli to get a coffee, a breakfast sandwich, and a lotto ticket. He doesn't have much, so he rarely splurges for a big ticket, but after spending thousands of dollars over the years on lotto tickets, he hits the jackpot. When given the choice of receiving the prize over 26 annual installments or in a lump sum, he goes for the lump sum. He wants to see $3 million in his bank account. Having been a kid who didn't know if there would be hot water when he turned on the shower, who was made fun of for wearing hand-me-down clothes two sizes too big, he decides to show everybody what he never had. He buys a house, a beautiful car, and a boat, and he meets his wife. He buys his parents a new house too. He lives from one extravagant vacation to the next. He donates money to neighborhood communities. In five years, his bank account is at zero. He sells the house, the car, the boat. His wife leaves, and eventually he goes back to work, and to a different deli.

The man concludes, *Money can't buy happiness.*

A single mother works two jobs to raise her kids. She can't remember the last time she wasn't working, cooking, or cleaning. Each month the bills pile higher, and each of those white envelopes with the glassine window she pulls out of her mailbox is another moment out of thousands when her heart sinks. There's no payoff. And as retirement looks more and more like a fairy tale her parents told her about, she cannot see an end to it all.

The mother concludes, *Money is our prison.*

A young man takes a job working for a company he doesn't like, selling a product he doesn't believe in, talking without joy or enthusiasm to potential customers. He suffers at work, fails to make income, and struggles to pay his bills. Over time, he loses his self respect, his family, and his health.

He concludes, *Money makes us greedy.*

A woman goes into business for herself. Not knowing her own hidden beliefs about money and success, she pours all her savings and all her loans into her business. As it fails, she borrows more, taps out her credit cards, and fights to survive. Without an awakening, she goes bankrupt.

She concludes, *Money makes us poor.*

But are these well-meaning souls concluding facts, or beliefs?

Far too many of us are believing what we think are truths, when in fact they are shared beliefs that don't hold up under deep thought.

Beliefs create our reality. They influence what we see. They filter out facts. And many of us end up thinking we need to struggle, starve, and wish for a better life.

Yet in these many moments so many of us share, we look upon the other side with envy. People who've found a way to unshackle themselves from the bonds of money. We think people who shun money are better than we could ever be. We feel shame that we cannot be so bold. There are those courageous souls who, in a moment of divine instruction, quit their jobs, sell their homes and all their belongings, and take off for a journey without knowing when or how they will return. Without the threat of money snapping at their heels.

We admire their courage.

We see the spiritually devout who embrace a life of poverty and give their souls to their God and the greater good. They spend their lives without a hint of luxury except for the greatest luxury of freedom and soulful purity. They are walking gifts of selflessness. They toil in war-torn countries, helping those in the most desperate and despicable conditions, unmoved by the threat of the warlord waiting around the corner for a new body to snatch.

We admire their purity.

We see the poets, the artists of legend, who romantically refuse money to instead wed their divine muse. They suffer poverty, the scant food or clothing, and the threat of eviction for the absolute thrill of following their passion. Their passion . . . what a delicious idea to devote oneself to such a worthy cause. Passion unbridled by what the rest of us suffer every day . . . want and need. These lofty spirits have no want or need. It's as though they drink the air, soaking in the sun, and find all the life-sustaining nourishment they need, like wild vines faithfully stretching up in reverence to the sky.

We admire their tenacity.

And here we sit, mountains of bills to our left as we stare off longingly to the right at these brave souls stretching free in a world without financial worry. They may suffer. They may struggle. They may spend days with hunger . . . but they're free. They are bastions of passionate living. They are the embodiment of what it truly means to be alive. They are living life to its limits. They are possessed with an unbridled mission. They are the true servants of the divine.

But what is the most insidious belief of all?

What is the hidden belief that keeps most of us in the dark about money?

These stories of the greed-tainted soul and the passion-inspired spirit are as old as money itself. In fact, perhaps the most famous saying that spread far and wide through our society is an ancient quote from the Bible. You can complete it on your own: "Money is the root of all ——."

You know the word. It's in your unconscious and now in your conscious. Whether we're Christian or not doesn't matter. That quote has permeated the secular world with force and longevity. The devil incarnate, folded patiently in your wallet, is waiting to taste the light and torture your soul once again.

But the Bible is misquoted.

These seven ageless words—money is the root of all evil—are fraudulent.

The actual quote from the Bible paints a very different picture: ". . . those who want to get rich fall into temptation and a snare and many foolish and harmful desires which plunge men into ruin and destruction. For the love of money is the root of all evil, and some by longing for it have wandered away from the faith and pierced themselves with many griefs."—1 Timothy 6:9–10

And here we taste our first tease of awakening. Not the Biblical kind, but the universal kind.

The love of money . . .

The love of money is the root of all evil . . .

And truly Awakened Millionaires aren't in love with money.

They use it. They appreciate it. They leverage it. But they aren't in love with it.

While this doesn't dismiss the acts of greed and corruption that some men and women have perpetrated on money's behalf, it does beg a question loaded with a new vision.

Is money the root of this greed and corruption?

Is money the cause of all our pain and suffering?

Is money the demon behind our cursed wants and needs?

Is money the sole force responsible for such collective misery and struggle?

Or could it be something else entirely?

What if we considered it to be what it is: an inanimate object? A piece of paper? A disc of base metal?

What if we could strip away all our notions about money? What if we could put down our negative thoughts about it, as well as our voracious desires for it?

Could we completely transform our relationship with money? Could we imagine a new future devoid of such a bizarre, schizophrenic battle raging in our heads?

Now what if we considered that this absolutely counterintuitive perspective on money led to greater happiness, truer success, and opened up our lives to abundance?

Could that be possible?

I'm here to tell you that it is. It is possible. It isn't fantasy or utopian delusion. And it isn't about awkwardly sticking our heads in the sand.

In fact, a healthy model for how we can relate to and interact with money is alive and well, instilled in a small group of people. It is a reality championed by this quiet breed of visionaries and passionate purveyors of good.

It is here. Now.

Meet the Awakened Millionaire.

CHAPTER 2

Awakened Millionaires

What we really want to do is what we are really meant to do. When we do what we are meant to do, money comes to us, doors open for us, we feel useful, and the work we do feels like play to us.

—Julia Cameron

Vash Young—You probably never heard of him.

But in the early 1930s he wrote one of the most influential self-help books of the time: *A Fortune to Share*. Young made a fortune in the life insurance business—during the Great Depression, mind you, when others struggled and starved and some committed suicide—and wrote his books to teach people how to care about others, be happy now, and truly serve. His books are still readable and relevant today, though Young has long gone.

Bruce Barton was once called "the man everybody knows."

An early "Mad Man" who was not mad. He was a popular advertising genius, cofounder of BBDO in 1919, one of the largest advertising agencies in the world, and a best-selling author, as well. His books, such as *The Man Nobody Knows*, revealed Jesus as a businessman who took 12 people and transformed the world. My own book on Barton, *The Seven Lost Secrets of Success*, reveals a man in love with principle over profit.

Mary Kay Ash: "A mediocre idea that generates enthusiasm will go further than a great idea that inspires no one."

She inspired women. She awarded pink Cadillacs for top sellers of her beauty products. She was on a mission to make a profit from her passion to help women find their independence.

Allen Carr tried to stop the world from smoking cigarettes.

Carr had been a chain smoker who discovered and developed a "talking cure" that worked. He spent the rest of his life teaching his Easy-Way method to the world. Celebrities to regular folks next door heard his presentation and stopped smoking. Ironically, Carr died of lung cancer. He allowed smokers to listen to this talk, smoking as he spoke. As a result, he breathed second hand smoke and became ill. When he learned of this, Carr said, "It was worth it." His message was that important to him. He was on a mission.

Debbie Ford: bringing light to dark.

She wrote books that awakened people to their hidden weaknesses, so they could regain their power and achieve their dreams. *The Dark Side of the Light Chasers* helped people who were deceiving themselves to see their hidden beliefs and break free. She appeared on television, in movies, and spoke around the world, to people everywhere.

What do they have in common?

They were all Awakened Millionaires.

They don't have an organization or a club. They don't swarm together for annual summits. They don't have a term for themselves. In many cases, they may not even be aware of what they are.

They just are.

These practical visionaries live by an odd creed . . . only odd because we'll be startled by its formula. It is a complete break from what we've considered fact with such tired conviction that we see nothing but dense fog.

The formula is simple.

Soul + Money = More Soul + More Money

Soul plus money, equals greater soul and more money.

Our first instinct is to reject this formula entirely.

The love of money is evil. Money destroys. It corrupts. It blinds. It certainly does not enhance the soul. What we consistently observe is that money kills the soul.

But . . . to consider that money and soul not only work together in harmony, but yield more of both as a result seems like madness.

Yet, we have living examples of this way of living, this very different relationship with money, this vision of passion and purpose.

We have the Awakened Millionaires—and each step they take reinforces this formula.

They are not supernatural creatures. They are not the heroes of legend. They live very real lives that might seem simple or unexceptional to the casual observer. But it is when we peel back the layers that we see the inner workings of this new paradigm waiting for the rest of us.

It is not the love of money that drives them. It is a singular vision.

It is not the desire for more money that inspires them. It is the desire for sharing their passion.

It is not the grounding of comforts that holds them steady. It is the grounding of purpose.

It is not the light of shiny objects and flashy new toys that guides them. It is the light of a mission.

This may read like the laundry list for a saint, but this is not about sainthood.

Awakened Millionaires have some form of spirituality at their core. Whatever form that spirituality may take stems entirely from the individual, as it must. Whether they connect themselves to a specific higher power, or have some sense of something powerful outside themselves.

It may or may not be connected to religion. More often than not, the Awakened Millionaires have their own connection to the Great Something that is unique to them. They have a personal relationship with their own sense of source.

Where they walk, they are in church.

When they speak, they are praying.

When they work, they are practicing devotion.

Again, each person decides what their spirituality is, which may or may not include participating with a particular religion. Being awakened, they realize that they *are* the spirituality they seek.

Awakened Millionaires are not just soulful beings. Awakened Millionaires are soulful beings who wield money *as a tool* for executing their mission.

Money, a tool of the soul.

Money, a collaborator with the soul.

Money, a funnel that directs the broad light of one's soul into the tangible world, with tangible consequences.

While Awakened Millionaires find that money flows to and from them with ease, they do not earn and spend for themselves or their family alone. Behind their passion, behind their purpose, and behind their mission—actualized with money and execution—is a solemn awareness that they can now accomplish what drives them.

Our passion is the strong, amorous feelings stirring within us. It is our profound desire.

Our purpose is not simply what we want, but touches on the reason for our existence.

And our mission is a profound purpose accompanied by a passionate conviction. It is our calling.

Passion + Purpose = Mission

Our collective relationship with money is bringing us down. This love and hate, and the sparks that fly when they dance, does not just hurt the individual who suffers. It ripples out, like collateral damage, to those around us, to the community, and to the society as a whole.

Some millionaires of the world today may have a passion. Yet some have a passion for money and for little else. For them, unfortunately, the negative stereotypes about money frequently apply. Their corruption, abuses of the law and people, and their greed are often the root of our visceral opinions about money and how it affects us.

Awakened Millionaires see far beyond this.

They are awakened to their purpose, their passion, and their mission, and their prosperous relationship with money follows suit.

Let us be clear: we don't need to be a literal millionaire to become an Awakened Millionaire. We might have millions in the bank. Even billions. Or we might have a thousand. We must look to ourselves to understand what prosperity means to us, as individuals. We must imagine prosperity holistically. Abundance does not and should not just refer to finances. Only we know what will give us meaning, joy, and a sense of prosperity.

So why use the term millionaire at all?

Because millionaire is a concept. A metaphor. The millionaire has long been our society's obsession, the ultimate symbol of someone who has it all. Someone we want to be, lust after, harbor jealousy towards, or outright hate.

We must take back the word *millionaire*.

We must strip it of its unhealthy money taint, and paint it anew with a deeper purpose, one that lives up to what money can truly become. We will let it become reborn as an inspiration for us. The awakened millionaire who sets off to make as much awakened money as they can to bolster the impact of their passions.

Soul + Money = More Soul + More Money

This is the new rallying cry—not for battle—but for prosperity in every sense.

CHAPTER 3

One Awakening

If a person gets his attitude toward money straight, it will help straighten out almost every other area in his life.

—Billy Graham

A true story of awakening:

The United States in the 1960s was not an easy time for many. Working on the railroads, the boy knew hard work from a young age. His father was the type to never skip a day of work. He put his son to work when he was five years old. Any time he wasn't in school, he would work on the tracks. It was rewarding in its way, as he got paid a dollar an hour and got a free lunch, but hardly the stimulation the young kid wanted.

His rural town in Ohio wasn't much to talk about. William McKinney had been born there. And the public library, a memorial to the U.S. president, was a tourist attraction. His family was deeply rooted in working class values. He saw the suffering and misery on the faces of his fellow locals. He heard the stories when neighbors would stop by for a cup of coffee or after work for some homemade wine. Everyone struggled.

The fuzzy family television told similar stories. Even hit comedies like *Gilligan's Island* innocently programmed people to think rich people were greedy and not likeable. And top shows like *The FBI Story* taught that people do horrible things in the pursuit of money. Other TV shows, like

The Rockford Files, conveyed the idea that money corrupted. The programming was insidious, but few noticed. After all, it was simply entertainment.

From a young age, he knew he wanted to be a writer. Part of it was the mythos around the writer's life—the adventures impervious to the doldrums of most people's lives. He read books by and about Jack London and lusted for the wild life. Traveling far and wide, experiencing exotic cities, and tangling with fabled monsters were captivating thoughts that could barely fit in that small-town boy.

But part of it was his desire to give joy. He wanted to make people feel better. It's hard for a young child to understand the complexities of the whats and whys behind people's suffering, but the long faces and smell of sadness was easy to understand.

He wanted to make people happy.

He wanted to write comedy, or humorous plays, to make people smile. He wanted to write books that inspired people to reach for a happier life. He was tired of seeing the doom and gloom, and feeling his own sadness at the struggle of life. He wanted to make a difference with his writing.

The writer's itch spread deeper within him as he grew older. The weight of the world around him made that itch spread faster. He didn't know what it would look like, what he'd write, but he knew he wanted to write. And he knew he wanted to make people happy. Seeing the horrors of the Vietnam War broadcast into everyone's home. Witnessing the civil rights struggles right on national television. Experiencing the trauma of a beloved U.S. president, a senator, and a leader of peace being assassinated were almost too much to bear.

Being young and unschooled in the ways of the world, he didn't know how to accomplish his goal. He went to college, but hated it. He failed nearly every subject, except the ones on American literature. There, he shined.

He put himself through a self-study program, reading biographies of authors, devouring books about writing. Because he was interested in human potential, he also read about self-help, psychology, hypnosis, philosophy, and metaphysics. Books like *The Magic of Believing* changed his life, teaching him that if he just believed, he could accomplish anything. Even being a writer.

He continued to work weekends on the railroad, hating the labor but enjoying the pay. He saved a small fortune for a kid, nearly $2,000, working on the rails. He said his goodbyes and jumped on a three-day bus to Dallas, Texas. Why Dallas? Because he loved the Dallas Cowboys. They were his favorite football team. And TV shows like *Dallas* made the city alluring.

He was not prepared for the intensity of a big city. The hustle, the speed, the diversity, the fury.

Dallas dug in hard. Work was hard to find. Friends were even harder to find. He was a likeable guy, outgoing, with a whip of a sense of humor. But he felt invisible. No job he got would stick. He made no friends at work. It was a struggle. And it almost broke him.

One day, after being in Dallas only weeks, with only $1,000 left of his hard-earned savings, he saw an ad for high-paying hourly work in the oilfields of Alaska. An adventure, good money, and hard work. He knew how to work, he ached for the adventure, and the money couldn't be better timed.

He went to the recruiting office and handed over the final $1,000 he had to pay for both the trip and the opportunity. His nerves bristled, but he was excited. Alaska was a bold adventure calling his name. He put all his chips, all his money, on the gamble of high-paying labor. He planned to work for a year, save money, and return for a sabbatical of writing. It was a bold, well-reasoned plan to implement a dream.

It never happened.

The company went bankrupt. His last $1,000 trapped behind their shuttered doors. Nobody answered the phones, no address was listed, and his money was gone. Later, he learned that the owner committed suicide.

It started as shock. Then disbelief. Which then turned to anger. And then panic. And finally an inescapable desperation.

What now?

All the hours of hearing his neighbors back home spill their sob stories about life's struggles hadn't prepared him for the reality of it. He knew he could go back home. His parents would welcome him, even if with the unbearable "I told you so" that was bound to come.

But he couldn't. He couldn't go home. He had to move forward. He had to get through this. He had no idea how, he had no money, and very quickly, he had no home to sleep in.

The next 15 years of his life were shrouded in poverty. He spent several months as a homeless man, sleeping on church pews, the Dallas post office steps, in the public library, and on benches at the train station.

The train station was the hardest. Working the railroad was the source of his early strength, his convictions, his wild imaginings, his work ethic, and the money he used to set off to claim his adventure, his success as a writer, and his chance to make people happy. Now the tracks simply taunted him. They said nothing. But they saw him. They knew he had failed.

Harder and faster he plunged. He watched as his soul, once a mighty block of marble, was slowly chipped away as if by the hand of a careless sculptor with no vision.

He felt hopeless.

He got off the streets by saving a little money from odd day jobs, hitchhiked out of town, and migrated to Houston. The big city was a boomtown in the late 1970s and early 1980s. You could get a job doing manual labor in the morning, quit it if you didn't like it, and get another job in the afternoon.

The dreaming writer did this. He took countless jobs, some of them so unfitting for him that he cried on his way to work. Along the way, he married a woman just as alone as him. Together, they struggled. They took turns working. Sometimes she worked while he wrote. The woman became an alcoholic, had to be hospitalized, and began the long journey of AA meetings and healing. She didn't drive at the time, so the writer-to-be drove her and attended almost every meeting. It was a nightmarish time, but they endured.

Over the years, the writer got published. He saw a play he wrote produced in Houston. He made no money, but received a taste of success. Cover story feature articles were published in national magazines. They paid little, but they built confidence. His first book came out in 1984. He made nothing but it was a personal milestone.

As he persisted in pursuing his dream, lucky breaks came about. Someone he met introduced him to a wealthy businessman. The writer was paid well to ghostwrite his book. Then the Internet came along, and the writer put his words online. Things began to speed up. Success, a little bite at a time, began to come his way. The sun began to shine. As years passed, he became more known, had more books published, and was invited to be in a movie called *The Secret* that changed the world.

Why? How?

In the deepest moments of desperation, where our souls are trapped in a viscous, primordial sludge, there is no momentum. There is no movement. All appears to be locked in darkness. Sadly, some rot away in this thick desperation.

But if not, what pulls you out? How do you escape? It takes a supernatural force, one buried within us. The same force that drives the Awakened Millionaire. The same force this young man used to finally escape and prosper.

Passion. Purpose. Mission.

His passion was to be a writer. His purpose was to make people happy. Together, they form the existential mission that finally pulled him from the sludge. It took years. Years of work, years of effort, years of dedication.

But he did it. He became the writer. He made millions of people happy. And even though money wasn't his main goal, he made millions doing it.

When he was poor in Houston, his wife broke a jar of tomato sauce intended to be their special meal for the week. He didn't have the dollar in his pocket to buy another jar.

He now has millions of dollars—enough for a sea of sauce if he wanted. But even with his prosperity, his passion is the same. His purpose is the same. His mission is the same.

He wants to write and he wants to make people happy. He is living the creed of the Awakened Millionaire.

He wanted to profit from his passion.

He wanted to profit by making a difference.

He wanted to profit by helping, serving, inspiring, and transforming. And he did.

Today, he lives his mission.

This is my story.

I tell it for a simple reason: Both you and I are of the same flesh and blood. We share the same human condition. And whether your story is like mine or not is irrelevant. I came from the depths of poverty and despair. I've tasted the worst of the worst. I went through the dark night of the soul. And here I am.

And my path to the Awakened Millionaire is one of many.

To the person who doesn't yet have a clear vision of their passion, purpose, and mission, you can find your way to become an Awakened Millionaire.

To the person who is filled with passion, driven by purpose, dedicated to a mission, but hasn't found the way to execute, you can find your way to become an Awakened Millionaire.

To the person who has tried and tried and tried . . . and failed and failed and failed to bring life to their passion and purpose, you can find your way to become an Awakened Millionaire.

To the person who already experiences financial prosperity, but who lacks the passion, purpose, and mission, you can find your way to become an Awakened Millionaire.

No matter what path we come from, the creed of the Awakened Millionaire, the path of the Awakened Millionaire, and the vision of the Awakened Millionaire is ours for the taking.

If we all gathered in one place and shared our stories, those stories would be a wild and unpredictable mish-mash. But no matter our starting point, no matter our challenges, no matter our passions, no matter our visions, the path to becoming an Awakened Millionaire is a path we all can follow.

Because it is simple in its very origin. The path to becoming an Awakened Millionaire is uncomplicated, but it does have four pillars that it must be built on. They are:

We must awaken our passion.
We must forge our purpose.
We must activate our mission.
We must embolden our relationship with money.

CHAPTER 4

What's Real?

Money is neither my god nor my devil. It is a form of energy that tends to make us more of who we already are, whether it's greedy or loving.
—Dan Millman

O ur understanding of money is an illusion. Our assumptions about the soul of money are fraudulent. They are as fruitless as firing bullets into the trees of an imaginary enemy of our own design.

The Awakened Millionaire knows that money is neutral, but a powerful tool in the right hands. It is a spiritual tool in the Awakened Millionaire's hands.

But sadly, the war on money is our birthright. The schizophrenic love/hate paradigm lies so ingrained within us, one would think it almost genetic.

But it's not. It's learned. We're educated to have a dysfunctional relationship with money. We're saturated with violent attitudes towards money. They are reinforced for us every day by everyone around us who shares the same attitudes.

We do not hear unadulterated appreciation and respect expressed about money by someone who doesn't have plenty of it.

This toxic relationship surrounding us has tragically become a new thread of the human condition.

It must stop. It must stop now. And it must stop with us. For this toxic relationship with money isn't static. Younger generations will inherit a purely dysfunctional relationship. Just as physical abuse may be carried down from one generation to the next, simply by way of example from a parent, attitudes about money are carried down as well. All it takes is one child to say "No, I will not be this way," for the insidious inheritance to come to an end.

This must stop for all of us. We can. There are people out there who have proven it's possible.

There are those who break this vicious cycle.

There are those who see the collateral damage and remove themselves from the battlefield.

There are those who find a way to transform their relationship with money.

These are the Awakened Millionaires.

They were born into the same world as everyone else, and into the same relationships with money. But they have pulled back the veil and seen the horrid reality of their inheritance: Money is neutral!

It's difficult to imagine how we can let go of all our fantasies about what money is, and accept that it is neutral. One way is to imagine how humanity managed to function before currency was invented, and wrap our minds around why currency may have been invented.

Until 1500 BC, all money was cattle, lambs, goats, or pigs. "Live" money was the means of trade. Right after that, the Phoenicians invented metal money. To make it more valuable, the metal became silver, copper, and, of course, gold. Later still, in 1656, Johan Palmstruch invented paper money. It didn't immediately take off, as coin was still revered and requested. Benjamin Franklin was instrumental in suggesting paper money be used in business. During his time, currency was accepted and became the norm in the United States.

Before currency, there were two types of economies: the barter economy and the gift economy.

In the barter economy, you had shoes. I had furs. I needed shoes, and you needed furs. We exchanged. The value of this transaction was clear-cut. There is no price tag on those shoes, nor those furs. Value is purely based on the need of the individual. It was an equal trade as long as both items are desired.

In another case, you may need my furs, but I do not need shoes. I still accept your shoes in trade because I know that I will be able to quickly trade those shoes for something else. It was a simple exchange, for very basic reasons. Nothing evil. Nothing treacherous.

The gift economy is much more complicated.

In the interest of keeping everyone in a community taken care of, services and products are given regardless of when or how they are rewarded. This is a culture that relies on customs and social norms of giving.

Even in the gift economy, we find questionable motives in giving. For instance, you might give a gift with the sole expectation that you will receive one in return. This has nothing to do with supporting the community at large, and has everything to do with forcing another community member to give you something in return.

There may also be a sense of obligation to present gifts and services to a particular lineage or kinship group, as we would to a royal family. This is a way of keeping reciprocity alive between your kinship group and the other . . . to keep a relationship of giving open for the future.

There are also forms of ownership in a gift economy. In the case of land, a property might be retained by a particular family, or lineage. It is simply established that they hold the use rights to that land. Only certain members of the community are granted usage of the land, while the land remains tied to the original owners.

Similarly, there are examples in a gift economy that are very similar to what we call intellectual property. These are like a copyright on a book. The book may be sold to individuals, but the content still belongs to its author.

It's easy to see why a gift economy can be complicated to navigate, perhaps even as complicated as current-day capitalism. There can be powerful groups, and those with less power. There can be those with more property, and those with less. And, significantly, debts are very real as well.

But let's look at the beliefs behind this.

If we were in a barter economy, and we tried to blame our problems on objects of trade, like shoes or furs, it would be absurd.

Would we make the statement, "Furs are the root of all evil"?

If we were in a gift economy, would we say, "Gift giving is the great destroyer"?

Of course not. So what, or who, should we be blaming for our life problems?

Maybe it has nothing to do with money at all.

One of the first recorded histories of currency was Anatolian obsidian, a raw material for stone-age tools, distributed as early as 12,000 BC.

The use of currency is that old.

Paper currency, as we know it, began in China in the eleventh century in the Song Dynasty in China. Merchants and wholesalers wanted to avoid lugging around bags of copper coins for large commercial transactions, so they began using paper notes to represent the hefty coinage.

Interesting that this simple solution to a problem became the source of one of our greatest enemies and our greatest love affairs.

Money is not the root of all evil. Money is the solution to natural phenomena . . . exchange of goods, and the "I owe you." You have something I want, I have something you want—let's work together. I'll give you this service right now, but I will need something in return.

So how did this transform into the contentious, complicated relationship we have with money today? It has nothing to do with money, and everything to do with people.

When people with questionable intent saw how money could become a form of control, we begin to see the rise of our complicated relationship.

I have the money, you don't.
I pay you, so I own you.
You owe me.
I want what you have.

There is an important and enlightening takeaway we all must see.

Spiritual and moral corruption started long before the rise of money as we know it. Members of our species have craved power, control, and luxury thousands of years before paper money came into being.

These are human traits, human flaws, human imbalances. Money was just a tool that clever people with questionable causes figured out how to leverage to advance their own agendas. Between the earliest record of currency, around 12,000 BC, and when that famous quote "for the love money is the root of all evil" was written in 62 AD, a lot of poor behavior must have gone down.

· And here we see a secret hidden inside the awakened millionaire's tool.

Money is neutral.

Once it no longer rules us, once we no longer rule it, a new stage is set for a monumental shift to occur. Opportunity is born, and many things that were once impossible become possible.

This can be done. We must do this once and for all.

And to do this, we must reintroduce ourselves to money.

We must look deep into the soul of money and realize that it has no soul. It is not capable of having soul. It is simply an object. We give it whatever soul it has. Our soul.

Money is neutral.

Money is an empty vessel waiting to be filled. Filled with what?

Our intentions. Our mission. Our passion. Our soul.

The Awakened Millionaire understands that money is a tool to make a positive impact. And we need more positive impact in this world.

That means we need a new awakening inside us as a people, when we realize that what is seen as our menacing master is destined to become the go-to tool good people use for passionate missions.

This is what we must champion. Now, through the end of our lives. We must acknowledge that what we have in front of us is, in many ways, the most powerful force for good we have at our disposal.

CHAPTER 5

Counterintentions

It's a kind of spiritual snobbery that makes people think they can be happy without money.

—Albert Camus

Our war with money is not just waged in our conscious minds. In fact, most of it is spurred by our subconscious and unconscious minds.

Buried deep within us are the learned habits, perspectives, patterns, and judgments we've inherited. And they turn into a behemoth standing in our way: blocks, limiting beliefs, and counterintentions.

Consciously you want one thing: money.

Unconsciously you want something else: money is evil so keep it away.

Since the unconscious is bigger, bolder, stronger, and in control, what it believes will win.

The mental blocks might be our inability to even imagine ourselves standing in awakened abundance.

They may be an inability to even consider a new relationship with money or a new truth about money's neutral nature.

They may be pure disbelief in a world where we are free from the evil touch of money.

It doesn't matter if we can consciously wrap our heads around it and accept these possibilities. If our subconscious minds are blocked to the possibilities, our subconscious minds will ultimately win the battle.

Limiting beliefs might have us secretly convinced we don't have the courage, the will power, or the follow-through to bring our soulful passions to fruition.

They may take the form of instantaneous subconscious doubt when we even consider the possibility of having a flowing source of money into our lives.

They may be the perpetual guilt of having failed and failed and failed, unable to carve out our own path to success.

They may be stellar objections to a world where we can be guided by a passion, purpose, or mission, let alone having them supported by the power we channel into money.

Counterintentions might take form as persistent self-sabotage, our subconscious minds dealing damage behind our backs through procrastination, hesitation, or restraint.

Why would we want to prevent ourselves from success, or block abundance?

One simple possibility is fear. Fear of the unknown. Fear of new responsibilities. Fear of success. Fear of failure. Fear of embarrassment. Fear of anything that isn't the cage we've been in all our lives, because we understand it so well, and it feels safe.

We could even have a deep, dark, secret desire to achieve money so that we can exact the same cruelty and control we've experienced at the hands of others wielding the power of money.

Whatever mental blocks, limiting beliefs, and counterintentions are lying in wait within us, we must realize that the simple saying, "I'm going to change my mind," will not always work. In fact, it usually doesn't. Our subconscious minds resent and resist our desire for change.

When we find ourselves firing bullets ceaselessly into a thick fog, we must tap ourselves on the shoulder, tell ourselves to lay down our guns, and take some distance to see the truth of exactly what war we've been engaged in.

We must transcend these barriers in new ways.

It starts with the number one cause of our subconscious barriers. It happens to be one of the largest causes of our war with money.

We feel we are victims.
We are the victims of outside forces.
We are the victims of powers we can't conquer.
We are the victims of circumstances we can't control.

But are we? Are we really so willing to give up our power so easily?

For when we live and act the victim, we relinquish control of our own lives and our own destinies.

We can't transform our relationship with money because we are victims of money's vast network of oppression.

We can't escape financial struggle because we're the victims of our debts, our bills, and our responsibilities.

We can't rise as Awakened Millionaires because we are victims to our hard lives and tough challenges.

Or at least this is what we tell ourselves.

To remain the victim is to close up shop and go home.

We've given up our power. We've acknowledged that we are at the mercy of the puppet strings attached to our arms and legs. We have no free will because we are the victims in a cage we never designed and never agreed to enter.

What a crippling, fraudulent idea. Almost as crippling as the tattered relationship with money we must change.

A mantra of victims is "It is what it is." It leaves little room for hope, change, or action.

People say it to shrug and give in to what they think is unchangeable reality.

What would be better than thinking or saying "It is what it is"?

It occurred to me like a flash of inspiration that this line would be more accurate and empowering: "It is what you accept."

In other words, reality is what you *accept*.

"It is what you accept."

Someone asked me about the phrase, "It is what I decide."

"Decide" could work, except it's not entirely true.

I had two friends die within a week, one totally unexpected.

If I could decide, I would decide to have them live.

I can't do that, but I can accept their passing.

"It is what I accept."

Instead of saying "It is what it is," say, "It is what it is *for the moment* and I am doing something about it!" and then speak what you want, not what you are giving in to, and act to make your new intention a new reality.

Surrendering is a high spiritual act when you are surrendering to your highest ideals; it's a poor act of victim mentality when you surrender to circumstances you honestly don't like.

I'll repeat that: Surrendering is a high spiritual act when you are surrendering to your highest ideals; it's a poor act of victim mentality when you surrender to circumstances you honestly don't like.

So many of us deceive ourselves with statements that at first glance look innocent—like "It is what it is"—instead of looking deeper to find what hides behind the statement.

I'm not suggesting that you deny reality or the facts you are facing, but I am suggesting that accepting facts as the final verdict is a poor move.

By accepting what I can't change, I still live in agreed upon reality while acknowledging my power in the acceptance.

It's a bit like the famous advice known as The Serenity Prayer:

God, grant me the serenity to accept the things I cannot change,
The courage to change the things I can,
And the wisdom to know the difference.

While most people associate the famous prayer with Alcoholics Anonymous, it actually came out of a struggle in politics against evil.

According to Susan Cheever, ". . . it may come as a surprise to learn that the prayer was originally conceived not as an antidote to addiction but in response to the barbaric evil of Nazi Germany that threatened civilization itself during World War II. Written during the darkest depths of the war by the theologian Reinhold Niebuhr, a first-generation German-American, the prayer captured the dreadful ethical predicament faced by Niebuhr and his fellow German anti-Nazi émigrés in the United States, who were safe from persecution but powerless to intervene against Hitler."

The wisdom to know the difference is the key. Too many of us give in without checking in. We don't use our wisdom.

Much better advice is from a Mother Goose rhyme from 1695:

For every ailment under the sun
There is a remedy, or there is none;
If there be one, try to find it;
If there be none, never mind it.

At least with this new slogan, you can sense that you have choice. If you are backed into a corner, you can choose to see options or you can choose to surrender. Either way, you get *to choose* what you accept.

Notice that the new line gives you more power; you may or may not use it, of course. Creating your own reality is all about choice and awareness. I am sure you will make the right decision to be the most empowered.

Whether you use it will depend on what you accept—but notice that it's entirely up to you. "It is what you accept."

Why do we remain the victim? Why are we so persistent and adamant about accepting these supposed chains and doing nothing?

Because we've grown comfortable. Too comfortable.

No, struggle is not comfortable and we don't like it. In theory, of course we want to evolve past these struggles. But we are resilient and adaptive creatures. We may complain, but we have adapted to this victim's life. We know our boundaries. We are sheltered from the outside world.

We have to understand that stretching for anything new will feel uncomfortable, because it's new.

Whenever you leave your comfort zone, you will feel uncomfortable. That's obvious, isn't it? But being uncomfortable isn't a sign not to proceed. It simply means you are leaving the known for the unknown. You are leaving your comfortable seen and unseen boundaries to move into unlimited power, wealth, and happiness.

The only way to get there is to allow the discomfort. After all, it's not a threat to your survival. It's only a step out of your comfort zone. It doesn't mean anything more than that. It is nothing to fear at all. In fact, feeling uncomfortable should be and can be a sign that you are progressing.

But there's another insight here: We are sheltered from the need to take responsibility. And that, right there, is the cure: Taking responsibility.

There are few conscious decisions that can work magic on the subconscious and unconscious mind. Few conscious actions that can make a dent on a realm of our minds that largely remains out of touch. It often requires subconscious reprogramming, like hypnosis, to dissolve these subconscious hurdles. Or deep mental-clearing exercises to slowly chip away.

Yet simply taking responsibility can have a powerful healing touch.

When we take responsibility . . . when we stand in the silence of our lives and quietly and humbly accept responsibility for everything we are, this decision permeates our being, soul and all. This is because taking responsibility is taking back control. It is acknowledging that even when outside forces bear down on us, we are not required to suffer soulfully or emotionally. That is our choice.

Here's another true story: A man started playing piano when he was four years old. He was a natural, yet his left hand never compared to his right. His right hand was twice as fast, twice as dexterous, twice as sensitive. He went on to study jazz at The New School, and graduate with a whole new perspective on music and improvisation.

A couple of years later, at 24, he was eating dinner with his parents in New York City. He shared with them some recent reflections he'd had on his old, unspoken difficulty with his left hand, particularly when playing the piano.

His parents finally told him that he was born with a mild case of cerebral palsy, which had rendered his entire left side weaker than his right.

This was an enormous revelation. Why hadn't they told him long before? They did not want him to perceive himself as having a handicap, or even a slight disadvantage. Indeed, he spent his life tirelessly working on his left hand's piano work, and discovering ways to compensate for it.

Now he sees it as a gift. His left hand will never be his right. It will never have the grace, the touch, or the breadth of movement. But the right hand will never have the personality, the odd swagger, and the clunky swing that his left hand radiates.

In fact, no one else around will have a left hand like his and no one will play music with the same twist. He sees it as a gift, not a handicap. His name is Mitch Van Dusen, a friend of mine who lives with inspiration and is helping me with the mission to transform people into Awakened Millionaires.

There are those born with far more challenging birth defects than he. Yet so many make the choice to live as fully as anyone else. Calling them miraculous is an insult to their incredible will to defy the expectations of their bodies and minds.

Another man had an accident when he was under five years old. He lost 80 percent of his hearing. Despite the difficulty of growing up while being taunted by other kids, and being considered slow or retarded by adults, he went on to great fame and fortune. He became a movie star, an inspiring bodybuilder, and a public speaker. Today we know Lou Ferrigno as the Hulk.

They didn't succumb to the victim mentality that many of us, with much less serious conditions in life, do so with such willing ease.

You may have a perceived limitation of body or mind, too. But it doesn't have to stop you or even slow you. It can be leveraged, appreciated, respected, and even loved.

Consider people born with every advantage you can imagine. Health, beauty, money. There are those who feel trapped by these wonderful circumstances. Fearful that their parents will consider their passions lowly, they feel they must fulfill expectations by taking on family business. They, too, miss out on all the potential they have, and blame everyone else.

Let us take responsibility.

Let us drown victimhood in the thunderous rapids of our own convictions.

Let us forever acknowledge that any complaint, any justification are excuses, and nothing more.

Let us never again succumb to this ridiculous idea that we have no power.

We have all the power we could need. We have the power to take responsibility. We have the power to reject the victimhood we're taught to accept.

We are not the victims of money; we are the commanders of our soulful cause with money by our side.

We are not the victims of debts and bills; we are the recipients of the services, the goods, and the opportunities that have enriched our lives.

We are not the victims of the here and now; even if it takes time and patience, we have the power to overcome any odds, any challenge, and any block that seeks to deter us.

We are not the victims; we are the authors of the stories of our own lives.

We are the champions of soulful money.

We are the Awakened Millionaires to be.

CHAPTER 6

The Formula

Earth gets its price for what Earth gives us,
The beggar is taxed for a corner to die in,
The priest hath his fee who comes and shrives us,
We bargain for the graves we lie in;
At the devil's booth are all things sold,
Each ounce of dross costs its ounce of gold;
For a cap and bells our lives we pay.
Bubbles we buy with a whole soul's tasking,
'Tis heaven alone that is given away,
'Tis only God may be had for the asking,
No price is set on the lavish summer;
June may be had by the poorest comer.
    —James Russell Lowell, *The Vision of Sir Launfal*, 1848

What happens when we scoop away and flush the gunk of victim-hood built up inside us?

We feel empowered.

We feel a profound shift from helplessness to grounding. Control of our destinies rescued from the thousand slave drivers we gave our power to.

It is uncomfortable to accept that we have been living as victims for years on end. No one likes opening their eyes and acknowledging how much of ourselves we've given up. It can be incredibly uncomfortable to finally see how deep the victim mentality has permeated every aspect of our lives.

Yet, the moment we take responsibility, the edge of this discomfort is blunted, as we become empowered, and we see a new realm of possibility.

We now have the power to discover, admit to, or transform. .. our mission.

We've touched on passion, purpose, and mission. It's important to understand them.

Passion is a deep love of something, or a profound desire.

Purpose is a goal, an aim, (and sometimes, but not always, it is the reason for our existence.)

Mission is a profound purpose accompanied by a passion. It is our calling. Our vocation. It's what we do.

Passion + Purpose = Mission

That word—mission—is intimidating. What kinds of things does the concept of a mission bring to mind? In a movie, the mission is to save the world from the bad guy. For a real-life mission we might think of a very worthy cause, like rebuilding homes in an area destroyed by a hurricane, getting people to Mars, or finding a cure for cancer.

Big things. Overwhelming things. Things that boggle the mind.

We must realize that these types of big-picture missions are executed through combining thousands, if not millions, of people who are on their own, much smaller, specific missions. No single person will be responsible for curing cancer. The cure will result from a culmination of countless studies, inventions, research, and trial and error, all happening around the world.

Eventually a cure will come to be, and while one group may be credited with a definitive discovery, humanity will have all those to thank who were working toward this momentous goal.

The truth is that mission, on the scale of an individual, can be something incredibly simple, and it begins with a passion.

Passion

This is the place in ourselves where the Awakened Millionaire is born.

Passion is easy. It's something we love. We love to do it. We love to study it. We love to think about it. We love to talk about it.

When someone brings it up at a gathering, we feel like we've finally found someone to have a real conversation with. We bond with others over mutual passions. Sometimes forging that connection is how we find our best friends, or significant others.

Our passion makes us happy.

Our passion thrills us.

A passion can be fixing cars. Cooking delicious meals. Tinkering with electronics. Making ceramics. Playing golf. Healing through touch. Plumbing. Taxi driving. Tasting beer from all over the globe. Trailblazing around the world. Cats. Dogs. Lizards. Pink flamingos. Lawn ornaments. Castles of Ireland. English gardens. Jumping out of airplanes. Flying airplanes. Flying remote control airplanes. Flying cars. Strongman training. Marathons. Scrapbooks. Books. Apps. Cooking. Magic tricks. Meditation.

Anything goes. Everything counts. Passion is immune to judgment. And any passion, with creative thought, can be turned into profit.

No one can look down on our passions. They are ours, and ours alone. They come from deep within us, and for reasons only we can understand.

We must embrace our passion. We must announce it proudly. Wear t-shirts about it!

Passion is what carries the Awakened Millionaire along through every step of a mission with sheer joy, excitement, and enthusiasm. Without passion, there is no mission, no journey. There is no purpose without passion.

Purpose

Every passion reveals a problem. When we love something, we want to understand it inside and out. Inevitably, we discover one of the following about our passion:

It's missing something. No book on a particular type of [x]. There needs to be a website about [x]. Couldn't there be an attachment to [x] that would do [y]? I've always wished for [x]. I can't find any information about [x].

It has a flaw, or a weakness. This could be improved upon. It could be better. It's too slow. It's too fast. It's too difficult. It's too easy. It is stagnant. There have been no recent innovations on [x]. [X] needs a revival.

Purpose is often born of these problems. For every problem there is a solution. It all begins with this simple question: What if?

"What if?" is a powerful question when asked in the right way. Most people use it to play out negative scenarios in their head: What if I fail? What if my idea bombs? What if I can't do it? What if I'm the exception to the rule?

Mindy Audlin, author of *What If It All Goes Right?*, calls those what if down questions. What you want to ask are what if up questions: What if I succeed? What if my idea is the winner? What if my next steps are the celebration turning points of my life?

What-if questions can be used to create solutions. *Not Impossible*, a book by Mick Ebeling, chronicles the inspiring stories of how he created solutions in record time by saying he would find a way, when none existed. He's famous for creating prosthetic hands for war victims by making the limbs out of a 3-D printer.

When Mitch Van Dusen and I would meet and discuss the Awakened Manifesto ideas, we what if upped ourselves into creating a movement and a mission. Our work became more than a book or an online product; it became a driving, passionate, all-fiery, inspiring movement.

All because we asked what if questions and the sister to it, "What would be better?"

Each of these what if questions represents a goal born from a passion. Each has been brought into reality. Each one, no matter how small, simple, or big, has changed the world forever, and each one will be built upon for future generations. That's how a mission is created.

A mission brings about positive change through a singular goal, fueled by passion.

The Awakened Millionaire has a mission fueled by passion.

Your mission is yours and unique to you. It could be to be the best mother to your kids, to be the best plumber in your city, to open a business that transforms lives, to market an invention that cleans water, turns solar energy into automotive fuel, or anything else. It is yours and yours alone.

Your mission is fueled by your passion. Whatever it is that you love, that you care about, is what you morph into your mission. As you read these words and meditate on your life, it will all become clear.

Onward.

CHAPTER 7

The Mirror

Lack of money is the root of all evil.

—George Bernard Shaw

Passion, purpose, and mission are the powerful forces of the Awakened Millionaire.

Most of us have no awareness of how deep our reservoir of passion truly is, and most of us have no understanding of what we can do with our passion.

Passion is a creative force. It can be harnessed and channeled in endless ways. It is the power behind every action the Awakened Millionaire takes, because it provides the direction, the focus, the purpose, and ultimately the mission for what we create in this world, what impact we have.

Ask anybody with a mission what they absolutely need to make their vision become reality, and they will all tell you the same thing.

A woman sets out to write a collection of short stories.
A man sets out to create new opportunities for affordable housing.
A woman sets out to build a girls' school in Afghanistan.
A man sets out to breed a rare type of orchid.

What do they all need to make their mission happen?

They need money. They need money for all the things they will need. They need money for supplies. They need money for offices. They need money for the infrastructure. They need money for promotion. They need money for building. They need money for employees. They need money, as a builder needs a brick, to bring their mission to fruition. Without it they can't, and they need money to live.

In reality, they need *creativity*, not money. They just think they need money. Since most people do, let's continue that thought.

Embarking on a mission is an investment of your time, your energy, your whole self. Many people begin a mission while they work a day job, or make money in a way that has nothing to do with their mission, but this is difficult to manage.

Many of us struggle with the idea that we don't deserve to be paid for doing what we love. This is a fantasy. Another falsehood planted in our minds.

We all deserve to be paid for doing what we love. We all deserve to be paid for bringing something positive into the world. After all, you have bills to pay; so do I. You should rightly charge for your work, so you can pay your needs. I should charge for mine, so I can pay for my needs. It's a fair exchange of energy, being paid out of mutual respect—and it's a lot easier than trading goats for shoes.

You'll notice a lot of mental confusion here, too. On one level, when you are struggling, all you think about is the desire for money. But when you finally have money, you worry about what others think, do you have too much, and are you corrupted.

Few recognize the tug of war in their mind: money is sought when they don't have it because they need it; money is shunned when they do have it because it triggers thoughts of it being evil. No wonder so many lottery winners end up broke after a short time. Their unconscious negative beliefs about money won out.

As Awakened Millionaires, we know better.

And here, in this light, we see money's true nature. It's simply a mirror. It reflects what you believe. In and of itself, money is meaningless—we project meaning onto money.

If we shift our relationship with money, transform our understanding of money, see money's true nature, dissolve our fears and hard feelings about money . . . then suddenly we can pick it up, hold it in our hands, and understand the simple truth: Money is neutral . . . until we give it meaning.

Money is a vessel to direct, elevate, and bring to fruition our mission, but we must dive deeper. It's one thing to reframe money in our conscious minds. We may taste the excitement of reimagining the possibilities when we wield the spiritual power of money. We may imagine the myriad ways we can fill this empty vessel with our own intentions. We may embrace this new relationship with money as we ascend towards a greater awakening, but that's only the beginning.

CHAPTER 8

The Mission

*Do not value money for any more nor any less than its worth; it is a good
servant but a bad master.*

—Alexandre Dumas fils, *Camille*, 1852

Walt Disney once said, "I want to make money from my movies so I
can continue making movies."

Note the purity in the statement. It's about the mission. His soul's
mission. Money is secondary. Money is the means to an end. The
relationship between his mission and money is symbiotic and cyclical.
One begets the other.

Disney loved cartoons. He knew that if they made him happy, they
would bring joy to many others who watched them. And he wanted to
make people happy. If we apply the Awakened Millionaire formula for
Disney, it might look something like this:

Passion: Creating cartoons and bringing others joy.
Purpose: Produce cartoon films for the public.
Mission: Bring others great joy by producing touching cartoon films for
the public.

Walt Disney is the perfect example of a man who was driven by
passion. His passion explicitly included bringing others joy, but when we
love something so strongly, we don't want to keep it to ourselves. It's

almost criminal to keep it to ourselves. We want to share it with the entire world. Even if we have the fears of putting ourselves out there, it is deeply ingrained in our soul's desire to radiate outwards.

At the grand opening of Disneyland on July 17, 1955, Disney said in his speech: To all who come to this happy place; welcome. Disneyland is your land. Here age relives fond memories of the past . . . and here youth may savor the challenge and promise of the future. Disneyland is dedicated to the ideals, the dreams and the hard facts that have created America . . . with the hope that it will be a source of joy and inspiration to all the world.

This is a mission statement. Disney's statement is as clear as day.

His success, his unstoppable drive is fueled not by money, not by success itself, but by one crystal clear thing. His passion. It gave him a vision. And it carried him along, guiding him every step of the way through his remarkable journey. He wanted to make an impact—and he did.

Regardless of the path that Disney's legacy has taken since his passing in 1966, his impact continues to ripple through time.

We must love what we do. Work done on what we love is no longer work. It is passion in action. It is joy. It is the reality of the Awakened Millionaire. Awakened Millionaires love what they do, and that love can change the world.

Money makes manifest the mission and purpose of our soul. Money is an ally to the soul. If we love what we do, then money is simply a tool to manifest it. They form a cyclical relationship in which one begets the other. In combination, mission and money can proliferate, and both become exponentially greater.

This is the foundation of the Awakened Millionaire.

This is the power behind the Awakened Millionaire.

This is the fuel driving the Awakened Millionaire.

CHAPTER 9

The Forgotten Penney

I resolved to stop accumulating and begin the infinitely more serious and difficult task of wise distribution.

—Andrew Carnegie

1902. A small town in Wyoming with a population of only 3,000. They were mostly miners. They made little money, and what money they did get was infamously spent in all the wrong places.

There were 22 saloons in this small town, willing to take the miner's hard-earned money on credit. This town showed little opportunity to the eyes of an entrepreneur. Yet, one aspiring entrepreneur had a passionate vision for his town, despite all the cards stacked against him.

Mr. Penney was a deeply religious man, raised by a Baptist preacher who taught him self-reliance as a young child. When he was eight, his father told him he would have to earn his own money for anything he wanted. Self-reliance was etched into him from an early age. This strict upbringing and early training in self-reliance made him sensitive to the needs of others.

As an adult, he was poor himself, with a wife and child to feed. But he had a mission. He wanted to open a store selling clothing at a discount, so that the people of his town could afford the quality clothing they deserved. No one believed he could pull it off. Every business owner, banker, and most of his family and friends questioned his sanity. On paper, his chances for success were dismal.

But this was his passion, and he used this self-reliant determination to take himself as far as he could go, whether it was an empire or a train wreck.

His name was J.C. Penney. His store? It was called the Golden Rule: Do unto others as you would have them do unto you. This was the philosophy he built his entire business model on.

His first store was a one-room frame building located between a laundry and a boarding house off the main business district in town. He and his family lived in the attic over the store. The store was furnished with shelves made from packing crates.

Unlike the 22 saloons in town, and plenty of other businesses, he refused to take credit on moral grounds. Everyone thought he was fit to fail. Yet, he made $466.59 his first day. His first year totaled $28,898.11.

To him, the Golden Rule represented more than just a marketing strategy. It was his spiritual conviction shared with the world. It became the credo of his business. He insisted on offering customers quality merchandise at the lowest possible prices. He loved people, was deeply religious, and made the people who ran his stores partners, not employees.

The strategy and the vision worked. People loved it.

At the end of 1912, there were 34 Golden Rule Stores with sales exceeding $2 million.

In 1913, the chain incorporated under the laws of the state of Utah as the J.C. Penney Company, Inc. Penney himself was opposed to the new name. He didn't like that it was all about him. But more importantly, it hid one of the founding pillars of his passionate rise to success.

His partners outvoted him. Yet still, Penney, the company and the man, maintained their spiritual vision to serve people.

In 1913, his company mission statement was:

To serve the public as nearly as we can to its complete satisfaction.

a. To expect for the service we render a fair remuneration and not all the profit the traffic will bear.

b. To do all in our power to pack the customer's dollar full of value, quality and satisfaction.

c. To continue to train ourselves and our associates so that the service we give will be more and more intelligently performed.

d. To improve constantly the human factor in our business.

e. To reward men and women in our organization through participation in what the business produces.

f. To test our every policy, method and act in this wise: Does it square with what is right and just?

Penney fought offering credit to his customers until the end when his partners eventually outvoted him. Penney didn't want to make a profit at the expense of his customers' well-being.

Nonetheless, Penney's disastrous business idea turned into a personal fortune of $40,000,000—even though his business model was not focused on profit.

He devoted his life to helping others, and not just with his stores.

In 1923, Penney established a 120,000-acre experimental farming community in northern Florida named Penney Farms. Some 20,000 acres were subdivided into small plots where industrious, moral, but economically destitute farmers could live and work until they could rebuild their lives.

In 1954, Penney established a second charitable foundation, the James C. Penney Foundation, which remains active today. This family foundation supports organizations addressing issues of community renewal, the environment, and world peace.

Awakened Millionaires don't just have missions. They want good for everyone they touch along their journey—from the people who receive their services, to the people who they employ.

Money does not just flow to Awakened Millionaires. It flows through them, and back into the world. This is a key part of the cyclical relationship in which soul and money beget more of one another.

Penney once said, "Give me a stock clerk with a goal and I'll give you a man who will make history. Give me a man with no goals and I'll give you a stock clerk."

J.C. Penney was an Awakened Millionaire in every sense. He was stalwart in his convictions, dedicated to his cause, and devoted to a single entity. Not profit, not his own self-interest, not the demands of his investors, but those he chose to serve. His mission.

CHAPTER 10

Stretch!

If money is your hope for independence you will never have it. The only real security that a man will have in this world is a reserve of knowledge, experience, and ability.

—Henry Ford

G row!
This is the internal command of the Awakened Millionaire.

To the Awakened Millionaire, growth is akin to breathing. We must breathe to live. We must grow to thrive.

Without it, nothing the Awakened Millionaire is capable of doing will have any sustained impact.

Because it's not just about our own personal growth; it's about the world constantly changing. There is no stagnation inherent in nature.

If we don't grow and adapt with the world, the world will leave us behind. We will be left standing there wondering where the wonder went, wondering where our impact has disappeared to.

We must grow. Always. Forever.

To the Awakened Millionaire, growth is a thrill. It is a calling in and of itself. It is a rite of passage. It is the soul of the Awakened Millionaire stretching outwards and forwards.

There is an indescribable fulfillment we receive when we look back and see the difference between us now, and us a day ago, a week ago, a month ago, a year ago . . . 10 years ago. Because the Awakened Millionaire is accelerating at a special speed, the growth becomes instantly visible.

This is one of the special perks of becoming an Awakened Millionaire. Growth is embedded in the fundamental formula we live each day:

Soul + Money = More Soul + More Money

That formula is an expression of pure, unadulterated growth.

When everything we do comes from a place of pure passion, purpose, and mission we want everything we do to multiply and proliferate. We want to spread our gifts and have a greater impact.

We want to take it to the next level. We want to get our message to more people. We want our love and passion to transform those around us. We want to be better, do better . . . and not just stay the same. We want to grow. That's how we make our impact.

This won't happen on its own, but the potential is there, ready and waiting.

To tap this potential, to grow exponentially, we must feed the soul, so that we can feed the mission. Like caring for a plant, we must fertilize the soil around it. If our mission is fueled by our passions, we must fuel ourselves.

We grow the self, the soul, and our passion. We seek new experiences to pull us forward. We search for courses and classes to educate ourselves. We find time to think.

Time to rest. Time to meditate. Time to exercise. Time to practice. Time to have fun. Time to listen.

In truth, we need to take this time to sharpen ourselves; to renew, rejuvenate, grow, stretch, learn, expand, and more. It is the way of continued expansion. No one knows it all. Persistent and passionate learning is the way to a better life, as well as more energy, joy, love, and enthusiasm.

As we feed the soul, growth follows naturally. It's magical. All kinds of things can occur when we feed the soul. And not just to us in our personal lives, but in our missions as well. Because they are directly connected.

What kind of growth can happen?

Improvement

We have a lifetime of improvements to make.

What is perfect? We say that there is such a thing as the perfect circle. But no circle created by humanity has ever been perfect. The only perfect circle is the concept of one that exists in our minds.

We shouldn't worry about perfect. But we can, and should, improve.

We've heard about the earliest electronic computers of the 1930s. They filled the better part of a room and did basic arithmetic. Today, we carry them in our back pockets and they talk to us, take pictures, and so on. Sometimes we may want to throw our phones out the window, but our lives are almost unimaginable without them. This is thanks to improvement. And as we know from ceaseless smartphone updates, the improvements continue.

To the uninitiated, this level of endless growth can be intimidating. A never-ending battle to grow seems like a nightmare scenario.

As awakened millionaires, we smile at the thought of that. Because, for us, our growth fuels our souls and fills us with meaning. It gives us joy and meaning.

Even in the moments when our self-improvement stretches us through discomfort, or exposes internal challenges that make us wonder . . . we embrace the discomfort. We embrace the wonder. We embrace it, because we know the fruits of our labor are worth every ounce of the stretch.

And we love the journey.

Because it's fun.

Because it's thrilling.

Because it's fulfilling.

Because it is empowering. Because we want to make a difference.

Reinvention

Reinvention is the hardest of all forms of growth. It is the most challenging, as it tackles the parts of us that have been etched deep into our minds, emotions, and souls.

On the face of it, it seems a nearly insurmountable task. When we have patterns that have been reinforced for years, if not decades, we have gut responses that immediately pop up. The power of the subconscious mind.

But here is where we must persist. We must persist every time the old way tries to stand its ground and save itself from extinction.

We must persist. And we will be rewarded for that persistence.

There is a special way to confront reinventions like this we can take from the Taoist philosophies in martial arts like Tai Chi. Tai Chi has a remarkable form of sparring called push hands.

Two people, standing in front of each other, poised in a deeply rooted posture, lightly rest the tips of their fingers on the other. Their mission is simple: push the other off of their balance so they take a step.

But it's not achieved by the way we think of pushing.

It doesn't use brute force.

It uses the secrets hidden in the yin-yang symbol common in Taoist literature. When your partner pushes with force, we don't meet with force. We empty ourselves—the exact opposite. Where your partner expects your resistance, you offer emptiness, and their own momentum topples them.

A complete transformation, an effortless victory.

When we reinvent ourselves, we don't fight it. We don't apply force. We state our intention, plant ourselves firmly on our feet, as if roots grew out of our soles into the ground, and sway with the wind, the rest of our bodies moving without resistance to the forces around us, like trees in a storm.

This requires advanced thinking and a mature spirit. The rule of thumb is, whenever you get upset, you've gone unconscious. That means a hidden belief was pushed and you reacted emotionally. This is how fights, wars, divorces, and more begin.

As Awakened Millionaires, we need to become highly sensitive to our own thoughts and behavior. If someone says something that irritates us, we stop and look at what is in us that got triggered. It's not about the other person or even what was said; it is about the unconscious triggered response.

The typical response is to push back with force: You hit me? I hit you back!

We don't do this as Awakened Millionaires. We empty and bend with the wind. When we empty, there is no force that can knock us over because we are not there to be forced down. Empty yourself and you will transform.

Discovery

Discovery, the third form of growth, is always the most fun. We look at ourselves and ask what's possible? What kind of Awakened Millionaire are we going to be?

While no Awakened Millionaire is ever the same, there are so many similarities that bond us together. And it is our journey into discovery that builds us into the unique powerhouses we're capable of becoming.

Think of us in our raw forms. Think about how much potential energy we have. Think about what we're capable of becoming.

When we put ourselves there, we begin to taste what it would feel like to activate greater depths of our potential. We begin to feel what that power would feel like. We begin to see the world the way our more powerful selves would see the world—and it feels good.

This is just one of the drives towards discovery. Behind it is the power of a single word: curiosity. Curious about tomorrow. Curious about how to solve a problem. Curious about how to profit from passion. Curious about creating, discovering, inventing new ways of being, seeing, serving.

When a man couldn't get a taxi to make it to the airport, he was curious how a service could be invented to be better than waiting endlessly for a cab. His curiosity created the app-driven, popular service called Uber. If you want a ride, tap the Uber app and a driver can be near you in only minutes..

In 2009, a driver was locked out of his car. He couldn't find his keys. He turned his complaint about lost items into a mission. He invented TrackR, a device that you put on your keys (or cat or anything you don't want to lose) and you can track it with an app you download onto your phone.

Behind every Awakened Millionaire is the desire to make an impact. A desire to bring good to the world, change to the world, healing to the world, elevation to the world, evolution to the world.

And we can. But how much? How far can we take our powers for good and transform them into tangible impact?

It all depends on what we're able to become. It depends on how deeply we commit to ongoing discovery. The more we discover about who we are and what powers we have, the more impact we can make. And I know that for every Awakened Millionaire, the idea of bringing more positive impact is enough, by itself, to push us into high gear.

How can we grow without first expanding our own horizons?

How can we have new ideas without continually educating ourselves?

How can we discover new in this world without the insatiable desire to explore?

Without the Awakened Millionaire's commitment to self-growth, there is a greater chance that we will become misguided, lose the path, or even leave ourselves open to corruptibility.

It's very easy to give in to temptation when it comes to money. Whether it's to take a job that we aren't in love with, or to skirt the edges of ethics or legality, being desperate for money often drives people to do things they regret.

One man accepted the assignment of coauthoring a book for an aspiring speaker. The man didn't believe in the book or the speaker, but he accepted the job for the money. Despite his intuition urging him to pass, he accepted. Within weeks the man became disillusioned, had an argument with the speaker, and parted ways. He also returned the money. Had he followed his heart, he would never have taken a job not in alignment with his own mission.

In our personal lives, in our businesses, at home, in our relationships, with our families . . . in all of it, we must be open, willing, and listening. If we do this, good things will come. Growth will come.

But we must come from faith, not fear.

We must grow, stretch, evolve.

CHAPTER 11

The Secret Ally Inside

Money is humankind's greatest invention. Money doesn't discriminate. Money doesn't care whether a person is poor, whether a person comes from a good family, or what his skin color is. Anybody can make money.
—Takafumi Horie

Intuition is our secret weapon.

While most believe rationality and critical thinking alone will propel them forward, the Awakened Millionaire dances their way to their objectives possessed with the spirit of intuitive improvisation.

We don't believe in the one way, or the correct way. We know that our path to success is carved in and of the moment, champions of inspired adaptation. We see the peak we strive to reach.

We see the fruits of our passions. We visualize the impact we will usher forward.

We do not travel blind, but we do not draw rigid maps. We do not build our empires with an instruction booklet, whether written in our hand or by the hands of others. There is no soul in the right way. There is no spirit in the only way. There is no adventure in the planned way.

Adventure is not just about the joy of it. Adventure is the embodiment of the intuitive dance, the flexible trailblazing of inspired improvisation.

Won't we become paralyzed by the need to make constant choices? At every fork in the road, must we sit down and weigh pros and cons?

No. Awakened Millionaires have a guiding light inside themselves. Because the Awakened Millionaire's journey begins with a passion, that passion serves as a lighthouse within us. It holds all the answers we need when the answers are not apparent in the exterior world.

Having this grounding center within Awakened Millionaires makes us the champions of speed. The soul likes speed. Money likes speed.

Going with the flow is an understatement. Thriving in the flow is the truth. The flow is constant. The speed is inspired, and improvisational intuition is our ride.

While consideration and reflection have their important place, they are not used in moments of indecision. They are carried out in the act of movement. When the moment of decision comes, when the fork in the road is presented to us, our intuition will have weighed the options consciously, understood the implications subconsciously, and made its decision superconsciously.

Stare at a list of potential ideas, one will pop out. That is our intuition guiding us. Sit quietly in the moment and allow our minds to wander. An idea will emerge. This is our intuition supporting us. Hold our passion close to us and look out into the world. Solutions and opportunities will seem to peel off in front of us. This is our intuition inspiring us.

Intuition is merely the inner decision maker that has a greater viewpoint than our conscious, thinking minds. Our conscious minds will slow us down. In a world that reveres the rigor of conscious thought, this might seem a rejection of what is sensical, even what is fundamentally us.

But this is a relatively new phenomenon championed in the West. In new and ancient traditions in the far reaches of our world, intuition has long been the guide, and we its progeny. Too many people worship intellect, not realizing intellect is never always right. Intellect is based on limited, available knowledge. It can't see all the options available for any one decision or desire.

Those who feel they know little of their intuitions when they embark on this inspired path are simply mistaken. Our intuitions have been alive, well, and active since our earliest moments of decision. We just have to listen. This is one of the reasons that we must allow ourselves time to enrich ourselves, to rest, to meditate, to think: so we can hear what our souls have to tell us.

This is not saying that we simply no longer think or no longer weigh options. Intuition is more holistically understood as the all-encompassing decision maker. Our intuitions consult every fiber of us, from what's inside us to the invisible antennae we have that read our environments every moment we're awake. Intuition is the governing body deciding the Awakened Millionaire's path. Improvisation is the expression of our intuition's decisions.

When we are in a state of action, our improvisational spirits show us what moves where, what words are spoken, and what vision is embraced. It is a conscious trance. It is enlightened progress.

Empires have been built on the shoulders of intuition. Famous entrepreneurs, investors, and leaders let their intuitions have the last say. Many times months of research, careful consideration, and logical decision making are scrapped at the last minute because of an intuitive hunch that rejects the whole notion.

Two jazz musicians sit down at their instruments together, an upright bass and a piano. They have no score. They have no chart. They have no rigid roadmap. They set off on an improvisational conversation. In the most awakened and inspired moments of this improvised music, we see a curious and awe-inspiring phenomenon.

In the exact same moment the rhythm of the bass shifts radically and the rhythm of the piano shifts radically in synchronous harmony. There is no score. There is no chart. There is no roadmap. There is no logical explanation of how one musician would know the improvised whims of the other. There is no logical explanation of how these two individuals, with all their individual quirks and tendencies, are locked in such a perfect articulation of shared intuition.

The music that emerges is not reactive, but reciprocal. Their conversation floats in between a dialogue and a shared monologue.

I do not know how this happens. I only know that it does. And it is the expression of our intuitions stretching beyond ourselves, building the in-tune paths we will follow and the inspired decisions we will make.

Even everyday conversation is based on trust and improvisation. When you speak over lunch, you have to listen and respond. There isn't a script. Their words trigger words in you. Your words trigger words in them. Where is the script? If you can make it through a talkative lunch, why not survive a day of moment-by-moment improvisation?

If we follow our intuitions, we follow the purity of our soul, as there is no greater expression of our soul's intrinsic, evolving shape than our intuition.

We do not access our full range of intuitive powers by trying to turn them on. We access these powers by letting go and giving in to the flow. We need not try. We need only be present. Our intuition will do the rest.

Yet, there are ways to amplify our connection with our intuitions. Our intuitions thrive on confidence and conviction, for in these states we find a bold silence and stability. When we make bold decisions, take bold risks, and throw in the spirit of adventure, our intuitions are empowered to stretch more, activate easier, and flow naturally through the curves of our lives.

Break your routines, and your intuitions kick in. Vary your route, and the flow kicks in. Engage your five senses, and your inner guide perks up.

But perhaps more than anything, the most fruitful activation occurs when we simply take a step, one foot in front of the other, without a thought of where we are going, or how. If you add an intention, such as being an Awakened Millionaire, then the radar in your brain kicks on and your intuition seeks out everything relevant to your goal.

Our intuitions kick in because we are purposefully devoid of too restrictive direction. We have no ideas to shape our next step, so our intuitions fill the void and flourish.

This may seem a bit like closing our eyes and jumping off a cliff. That's not entirely untrue—and it certainly beats stagnation.

We live boldly and bravely. We take risks. And we act quickly, without hesitation. We cannot succeed as Awakened Millionaires if we don't have the bravery to take on wild challenges. Do what no one else will do. What others may think crazy or dangerous.

We cannot succeed as Awakened Millionaires if we don't step boldly and act loudly.

We cannot succeed as Awakened Millionaires if we don't act with speed and consistency.

To the Awakened Millionaire, it is all part of the risks that are worth taking.

Never let those who don't understand get in our way. If they knew what we know, they would be right there beside us. But we cannot judge those who are not there yet, and we certainly can't let them slow us down. Be bold. Be brave. Take risks. And never hesitate.

Listen to yourself. Look around, and we see plenty of people offering step-by-step guides, this right way or that right way. There's nothing wrong with this, however, it usually only scratches the surface.

We don't find the translation of passion into profit through simple brainstorming alone. Yes, that is a part of it. But Awakened Millionaires leverage their secret weapon: their intuition. Buried in our minds, our souls, and our guts, are the answers we seek.

CHAPTER 12

The Sole Purpose of Money

If you work just for money, you'll never make it, but if you love what you're doing and you always put the customer first, success will be yours.
— Ray Kroc

Arnold Patent wrote in his little book, *Money:* "The sole purpose of money is to express appreciation."

Appreciation. Gratitude.

Simple ideas that we shouldn't reserve just for national holidays. What if appreciation wasn't just soul-nourishing? What if it was an integral tool for the Awakened Millionaire?

We must have gratitude for everything. We must appreciate the many blessings we hold dear to us, whether they be our family, our friends, our time, our passions, our communities, our homes, and our ability to feed and clothe ourselves. We know this, even if we don't practice this appreciation in our everyday lives.

Oddly enough, money has been blamed as an appreciation killer.

At times, we've struggled so hard to bring money in. But then we see it float right out through the slew of bills we must pay, the debts we owe, the mortgage, the utilities, the cost of food—it is as if money were a callous jokester toying with our happiness.

Money . . . a jokester?

Money . . . with a personality?

We, as Awakened Millionaires, know this isn't real. Yet this out-pouring of money to fund our basic survival seems to be one of the greatest sources of our frustrations. But what if a twist is waiting for us to notice it?

What if the monthly bills held a secret to making even more money? "The sole purpose of money is to express appreciation." What does that mean? That we gratefully kiss each bill we receive in the mail? That we write "Thank you!" on every check we send? We send flowers to the government for taxing us?

These are absurd notions to most, but they are a hidden tool for prosperity to the Awakened Millionaire.

When we send money to the gas company, the phone company, or the mortgage company, we are in fact expressing appreciation for what bounty we live with daily. We have a roof over our heads. Be grateful. We have a phone to keep close with our friends and family. Be grateful. We have a car to take us wherever we want to go, at any moment. Be grateful. We have a college education that transformed us. Be grateful. The sole purpose of money is to express appreciation, and every check we send off to pay a bill is an opportunity to express appreciation for what we have.

But this isn't just a glass-half-empty versus glass-half-full perspective. That doesn't even begin to touch on the power lurking in the positivity of appreciation. This is the difference between a scarcity mindset and an abundant mindset. This is the difference between the poverty mindset and the prosperity mindset. This is the difference between the victim mindset and the awakened mindset. It's only when we leave the scarcity, poverty, and victim mindsets behind that we see a startling truth.

Wrapped in these mindsets, we've been radiating out clear signals that we don't appreciate money, don't respect money, and don't understand money. Money goes elsewhere. Whether it's radiating out into the Universe or simply into our own subconscious minds, the vibration of scarcity, poverty, and victim mindsets is enough to squelch any possibility of awakening abundance.

As long as we unconsciously or consciously think money is bad, evil, or scarce, we will attract into our awareness proof of our belief. A person believes in conspiracy theories, and one day their computer has a virus that demands a ransom to be removed. A person believes no one can be trusted, and one day their employer lets them go. A person believes that money corrupts, and one day their partner steals their clients.

Gratitude and appreciation naturally wipe away these maligned vibrations within us. When we express gratitude, we open ourselves up to receive more, earn more, make more, and do more. We are telling every aspect of ourselves, and everything we encounter, that we are ready. We are ready to receive because we appreciate what we receive.

And not only that we are ready receive, but also that we are ready to give. This is key.

Receiving is just as important as giving; how else will the money come to you? Without acknowledging your self-worth, or the service you provided, money will not come to you. And when it does come, you must appreciate it for it to stay.

This is the cyclical flow of money.

Money is flowing around us all the time. There is no shortage of opportunity to tap into this flow. At any given time in the United States alone, there is over a trillion dollars flowing between us all. A trillion dollars in paper and coin, money we could put in our pocket, and we must know that it is coming to us if we remain open to it.

Do we really live in a world where money only goes to those who are clever enough to siphon off a share for themselves? Is it really only about knowing how to play the game and get ahead? Of course not. That is an antiquated way of looking at our economy.

A simple example is a restaurant we love to frequent. While there are plenty of restaurants in the neighborhood, we always end up coming back to this one. Why? Part of it is the delicious food (Italian, of course). Part of it is the price.

But it is often the intangibles that make us loyal customers, that make us want to come and offer part of our trillion-dollar share to this restaurant.

That intangible is often some form of appreciation we feel radiating out from the server or the owner. We feel appreciated walking in there. We feel it in the way they talk to us, the way they interact with us, the way they treat us like loyal customers or even friends. We sense the attention to detail. The flowers on the table, the lit candle, the little mint that comes with the check. It's all saying, thank you. The pull of this appreciation is undeniable. We come back for more.

It is a sign of a new economy that has emerged since our calamitous recessions and the struggles we've experienced as a society since the turn of the millennium. Amidst all the struggles and hardships, we see new trends in how people want to interact with businesses. We see a rise in independent businesses here in the United States. The combination of these—a shift in interaction and a rise of independent entrepreneurs—is prime groundwork for the Awakened Millionaire.

As if the struggle of the economic hardships only strengthened their resolve, these new entrepreneurs are in tune to the opportunities they see everywhere, opportunities sitting, waiting to be championed. These are the entrepreneurs who have built businesses when everyone warned them against it. These are the entrepreneurs that thrived on a conviction that self-reliance and communal engagement was the path to prosperity.

Take the bookstore. For the majority of the twentieth century, independent bookstores and libraries were the predominant form of literacy sharing. There were no megastores yet. There were no Internet giants.

But they came. Mom-and-pop stores that existed for generations were run out of business by Barnes & Noble. Barnes & Noble . . . the unbeatable giant. But then Amazon came along and forced many Barnes & Noble stores out of business. Admittedly, it's so much easier to just order online.

Then this new economy of self-starting, self-relying entrepreneurs began to emerge. Now, you find an independent bookshop opening up in your neighborhood. Not only that, they have a coffee shop inside as well. They make a great cappuccino.

Suddenly, it feels like a novelty to step inside and spend half an hour sipping a coffee, running your fingers down the pages of a book you've been curious about, and chatting with a stranger about it.

In an age of convenience, as we see with the Internet, we are seeing movements to bring back the real-life experience into our communities. The human touch. The warmth of reality. This is the prime economy for the Awakened Millionaire.

This is the time when opportunity, support, and resources for self-starting entrepreneurs have never been better. This is the time where we as a global community are gradually expressing and supporting a desire to connect more. Our world is ever changing, ever evolving. Change in inevitable—and the Awakened Millionaire adapts.

We cannot become fatalistic about a diminishing world with diminishing opportunity. We cannot engage a conversation about humanity losing its soul. We cannot succumb to an apocalyptic mentality about the big, evil corporations owning us for good. We must not be victims of the times or circumstances.

We must see beyond these distractions to focus in on the here and now. We must express our gratitude for what we do have, and let it guide us to the opportunities sitting right in front of us. As Awakened Millionaires, we must bring solutions to the world. We must bring opportunity to the world. To do that, we must channel our own self-reliance to seize the opportunity already waiting for us.

CHAPTER 13

Forget Selling, Start Sharing

People first, then money, then things.

—Suze Orman

For J.C. Penney, none of the conditions for a typically profitable business existed. Except in his mind. He had no perks that put him ahead, except for his passion to enrich the lives of those in his community. He knew that people deserved better, that people would agree, and that they would take advantage of what he offered them.

The struggling people of Kemmerer, Wyoming, walked into the Golden Rule store and saw fashionable, well-made clothing. Instead of immediate defeat, turning around, and walking out the door, the people could delve into shopping. They had confidence that they could afford what was in front of them. That was empowering. That gave pride. Wearing those clothes changed how a person felt walking down the street.

What's more extraordinary is that it didn't stop with what the people could purchase and how that made them feel. His employees were empowered too. Their direct involvement in the business made them enthusiastic, confident, and empowered—all the qualities the customers wanted for themselves. This created a positive relationship between the customers and the salespeople.

This is the profound power of Penney's business model. It created an overwhelmingly positive experience for those on both sides of the line: the buying side and the selling side.

We have a product, we have a service. Something good. That is where every entrepreneur's journey begins. We must get this impassioned product or service into the hands of the right people, the people who will benefit the most from it.

If we don't sell, if we don't market, if we don't promote, our business will remain in the basement, along with all our unfulfilled good intentions. Business is selling. We must sell.

Sell.

A concept perceived with demonic qualities as terrible as money itself.

Particularly for the spiritually inclined.

Too many believe that

Selling is sleazy.
Selling is sneaky.
Selling is dishonest.
Selling is manipulative.
Selling is unnatural.
Selling is ugly.
Selling is certainly not soulful.

These statements are too often true.

There are people who have despicably abused their selling savvy to cheat people out of their money. There are people who have preyed on the desperate to serve their own financial benefit. There are people who sell with no compassion, no understanding, no sensitivity, and no vision. There are people who lie, cheat, and steal to swing the sale. There are people who bend the boundaries of the rules to clinch the sale.

Isn't selling inherently disingenuous? Doesn't it taint the parts of our souls dedicated to a mission of giving? Isn't giving itself the ultimate expression of good with selling a tainted cousin? Doesn't it taint our passion, soil our purpose, and derail our mission?

No. That is not the case. The Awakened Millionaire knows the true nature of business.

Business is sharing.

Look at all the facets of the Awakened Millionaire's DNA—passion, purpose, mission, intuition, inspiration, spirituality, and ethics. The Awakened Millionaire wants to make it all happen, get it out in the world, and share it.

Selling, marketing, promotion—that's business. Business is how we share ourselves, our passion, and our products or services with the people who will benefit from them. It's how we manifest our mission, make it real.

Soul + Business = Sharing

We must know who will benefit. We must know where to find the people who will benefit. We must know how to connect with those people. We must know what to communicate to those people. We must know how to sell.

We could run up to strangers on the street and scream, "I can make you happy!" and they would simply ignore us, writing us off as a misguided soul secretly in search of a free dollar. It wouldn't matter what good we held in our hands. It wouldn't matter whether or not we could indeed save their lives. To scream in their faces with the hope they'll immediately understand how valuable we can be to them is profoundly ineffective.

To hem and haw and dance around the sell is equally ineffective. People distrust a lack of confidence. If we can't be compelling, they assume there must be something wrong with the product.

We live in a world rife with distraction, with bustling hustle, with people pulling for our attention, our interest, and our desires. Our senses are overloaded with input. There is very little room to communicate in a world with such noise.

So how do we talk to them? How do we communicate the benefit we offer to them? We must speak from the heart, from the soul, from the point of passion, with true understanding and empathy for the people we serve—our customer.

Few stressed this better than authors like Dale Carnegie. His 1936 masterpiece, *How to Win Friends and Influence People*, remains a classic today. His focus on the other person, not you, holds the key to how an Awakened Millionaire thinks and behaves. It's about understanding and serving the other person, not yourself. As a result of serving others, you will be served. He wrote, "Success in dealing with people depends on a sympathetic grasp of the other person's viewpoint." He also wrote, "Remember that other people may be totally wrong. But they don't think so. Don't condemn them. Any fool can do that. Try to understand them."

The famous sales teacher and author, Zig Ziglar, also pointed in this direction when he said, "You can have everything in life you want if you will just help enough other people get what they want."

The best copywriters know this. As I wrote in my book, *Hypnotic Writing*, "Get out of your ego and into the other person's ego." Focus in your writing and speaking on what the other person gets, not on what you sell or offer.

We do not say, "I have the best solution that will ever exist. My product is packed with this feature and that feature that blows away everything else. My product will change the very way the world spins." That'll happen about as regularly as the wheel is reinvented.

We say it differently. We say, "You have a problem. It affects you in this way. It takes away from your life in this way. It holds you back in this way. And I have a solution. It not only solves your problem, but it brings you happiness. It brings you a better life. It brings you more fulfillment in what you do."

Bruce Barton, cofounder of BBDO, the giant advertising agency, explained the difference between selling gasoline and selling dreams when he said selling gas was selling a product, but selling the end dream of being able to go on vacation or to work because of the gas in the car was selling the benefit.

It's the difference between saying here's a new computer with new high-speed bells and whistles (a feature) and here's a computer which will enable you to get your work done more efficiently (benefit). Always focus on the benefits.

We speak not just to their rational mind. We speak to their emotional core, to their deepest interest, desires, and pains. We resonate with their innermost beings.

We do this by stepping outside ourselves. By going beyond our own personal desires. Our motives must spring from the needs and wishes of our customers.

If we speak with integrity, with honesty, with passion, and with commitment to making a difference in their lives, then we see the soulful side of selling.

We must not forget that all of us are discerning individuals. We think for ourselves. We consider intelligently. We look at the options and we all have a decent intuitive meter that tells us when something is on point or when something is off and against our self-interest.

Yes, there are times when in our most desperate moments we will cling to any solution that has the remote possibility of saving us. But if we, as Awakened Millionaires, wear our integrity on our sleeves, if we speak with respect and dignity, then we never need to worry about the dark side of selling and persuasion. The inherent authenticity you hold will stand by your communication and speak to the authentic observer in your customer.

We must be champions of our passion and we must be champions of our product. We must believe we are providing transcendent value to our customer. For if we're not, we must step back and reassess what we are doing. If we are bringing the utmost potency of our passion, purpose, and mission, then we must do justice to this. We must get our products in the right hands and we must not let a fear of persuasion and selling get in our way. We are in the business of sharing.

CHAPTER 14

How Much Is Enough?

I've got all the money I'll ever need if I die by four o'clock.
—Henny Youngman

How much is enough?

At some point the Awakened Millionaire must come to grips with the idea of scarcity versus abundance. In the old view of looking at the world, scarcity is what drives people. They work to pay the bills. Because of issues with beliefs about money and success and worthiness, it is always a struggle. Rarely does one stop fighting through life to get to a place that one trusts enough to rest—most have to keep working.

In the new view of the world, there is more than enough. There is abundance. It's basically the same world, but the Awakened Millionaire sees opportunities where before he or she saw none. They realize that money, in one form or another, is available for all. It need not to be governed or restricted or dealt out. It's available, and following your passion is how you profit and receive your share.

But how much of a share do you need? How much is enough? Do you stop receiving money when you hit a specific number? Do you stop working when you achieve a particular dream?

The Awakened Millionaire realizes there isn't a cut-off number or a deadline for passion. As long as money comes in, they receive it and become a steward for it. As long as passion pumps through their veins, they continue doing work that feels like energetic play.

And as long as people are willing to pay for the service or product the Awakened Millionaire provides, then receiving it is the right corollary. Few respect anything given to them for free, so continuing to charge and to profit is the way of right business. Certainly the Awakened Millionaire may at times offer pro bono service. But it isn't given as a way to give back, as the Awakened Millionaire knows he or she didn't take anything to have to give back! If they give, it is out of an open heart and a willingness to share in certain situations.

But what about the spending and buying of things? The Awakened Millionaire knows that spending and buying are ways to keep the economy moving and giving work to all. When anyone buys a single dinner, they are contributing to about 70 people who helped make it. Not just the restaurant owner, but everyone from the wait staff to the cook to the farmers to the drivers who helped get the food where it needed to go to be prepared. A dinner becomes a stimulus to the economy—and so does every other purchase.

Giving has no limits, either. Giving is good for the soul of the one giving, and can be life changing for the one who receives. Without the giving of tycoons such as Andrew Carnegie, libraries may never have been available to awaken the lives of millions. Without the giving of others, good causes may never have been funded.

Programs such as Kickstarter, an online way to crowdsource funds for individual projects, are the new wave. A regular person maybe without education, experience, or enough funds, posts a request on Kickstarter. They tell their story and ask for money and offer some-thing, such as a signed album, in return. The public responds and donates money. The people behind Kickstarter get a percentage of it. It's a win–win–win. The person seeking funds gets money, the people giving funds get something for helping, and Kickstarter makes a profit. No one should put a ceiling on what the company should profit as a result of such spectacular service.

I often hear from people who think everything I offer should be free. They never seem to realize that their request reveals their limiting beliefs about money. Or that their limiting beliefs are the very reason they are struggling and wanting everything given to them. After all, when I offer a program such as The Zero Point, and I put a price on it, it's because it wasn't free for me to make it.

The reality is that the people involved want to be paid.

- Audio engineers want to be paid.
- Graphic artists want to be paid.
- Credit card merchants want to be paid.
- Manufacturers want to be paid.
- Warehouse owners want to be paid.
- Shippers want to be paid.
- My staff want to be paid.

And why do they want to be paid? For the same reason you do: Because they have their own bills, too.

So is it really reasonable to ask for a program like The Zero Point (www.thezeropoint.info) to be sent to you for nothing in return? Does that make any sense? Is that fair? Plus, most people don't value what is given to them as a handout.

I give away my book *Attract Money Now* at www.attractmoneynow. com. Have you read it? Have you implemented the seven steps in it? Be honest.

I also give away *all three* volumes of *The Miracles Manual* (www. miraclesmanual.com).

Did you go get them? Did you read them? Did you implement what you read? Tell the truth.

If you are serious about making a difference in your life, then stop asking for freebies and invest in your own awakening. It's the difference between free and freedom.

There will always be critics. Some in the world will say the Awakened Millionaire has too much. Critics will say that of anyone, of course, who has more than the critic. In truth, anyone can attract whatever amount they wish, and distribute it as they wish. There is no ceiling to income except mental ones. There is no limit to spending or saving or giving except mental ones. The Awakened Millionaire has to answer to his or her own peace of mind, not the peace of a critic.

Following passion, profit comes; by sharing the profit however one wishes, balance is created in the world. Since this formula is not limited to any one person or group of people, anyone can grasp the basics of living the Awakened Millionaire lifestyle and do with their money as they please. Then, instead of condemning those who have, they, too, can clean up their relationship with money and themselves and become an Awakened Millionaire, as well.

There is never too much wealth; there is only not enough awareness in how to receive and distribute the flow that comes in.

CHAPTER 15

Never Ever Fail Again

Never confuse the size of your paycheck with the size of your talent.
—Marlon Brando

There is another hidden agenda working behind the scenes, fouling our understanding and relationship with business and selling. We have to come face to face with it, or we will not move forward. It is our own fears of inadequacy, self-worth, and failure.

As with the concepts of money and sales, the Awakened Millionaire has an entirely different, counterintuitive understanding of failure from most people, and it's simple.

What are every entrepreneur's deepest, darkest fears? We put our product out there, and nobody buys it. Then we think the mission has no value. Our self-worth was an illusion. We have failed.

We put our product out there, and then we see another one that's uncomfortably similar. We think, there is too much competition. How can I contend with everyone else?

We put our product out there, people buy it, but they complain bitterly. Again, we have failed. I must have been wrong.

But we have not failed.

Awakened Millionaires do not have failure in their vocabulary.

There is no such thing as failure; there is only feedback.

Feedback is a beautiful thing to the Awakened Millionaire. Whether it comes in the form of happy customers, deafening silence, or a cacophonous uproar, it's all feedback.

The Awakened Millionaire welcomes every kind of feedback because it is the gateway to opportunity.

Feedback = Opportunity

Life is a big *Choose Your Own Adventure* book. Nowhere is that more apparent than when we look at how we each react to failure. The choices we make in moments of failure are some of the most impactful of our lives.

A woman is inspired to become a stand-up comic. She wants nothing more than to make people laugh. She practices her first routine a hundred times. She records herself, studies her timing, and tweaks her cadence, her emphasis, every detail. Her big night comes, and she's met with an audience of crickets. She is devastated.

She goes home, drinks half a bottle of wine, and goes to sleep. In the next few weeks, she talks to her friends about making some changes to the routine and trying again, but she can't face the disappointment one more time. She puts it off, and puts it off. She never gets back to another comedy club, and her dream is shelved.

Or she goes home, drinks half a bottle of wine, and goes to sleep. (There's no shame in a brief pity party.) The next day she thinks about the audience. It's painful to remember their unsmiling faces, but she forces herself to. Come to think of it, they were an awfully young crowd. There was a kind of post-grad vibe in there. It's no wonder they didn't get her jokes about being a single cat lady in her thirties. She decides to try another venue that has a slightly older crowd. It's nerve wracking, but she does the same exact routine, and gets laughs.

Or the next day, she asks a few friends to come over and be her captive audience. Her friends have a great reaction to the routine, but she figures, of course they do; they wouldn't tell me if I was bad. But afterwards, one of them says something she never considered. The friend says it took a while to get her sense of humor—it was so different from anything she'd heard. Maybe there was a way to prime the audience, give them an opportunity to get it before launching into the routine. She gives it a shot, and her next performance gets laughs.

Or the next day, she reaches out to the manager at the club where she performed. She asks him for his genuine thoughts on her routine. It's tough to listen to what he has to say, but she sees the truth in a lot of what he says, and realizes there were a lot of things she didn't pick up on by critiquing herself. She makes some tweaks in the routine and tries it again. This time she gets a lot of smiles and some light laughter. She talks to the manager again afterwards, who has nothing but encouraging things to say. He tells her to keep at it, keep making improvements. She does, and the manager becomes something of a mentor to her.

There is only one option to fail and give up in this story. There are many options to move forward, make discoveries, make changes, and shake things up. A million ways to move forward.

We get the opportunity to ask questions: What's next? How can we make this better? What can we tweak? Were we in the right place? Were we at the right time? What can we add? What can we remove? Are we talking to the right people? How can we turn this into something good? What is the hidden product or service?

These opportunities are the gifts our customers give to us. The goal of every mission is to give them value, to give them what they want or need, to give them our best. Through feedback, they tell us everything we need to know in order to do that. We only need to listen.

Back in 1984 a struggling author tried to sell a six-lesson course on how to write; he marketed it using a classified ad. He struggled to get the money for the ad. But he did. The ad bombed. Was it a failure? No. It was feedback. The young man took the six lessons, weaved them into a book, and it became his first published book. I know. It was my book, *Zen and the Art of Writing*. Seeing it published was a defining moment in my life, but it didn't come until after a failure.

Hit a roadblock, go around it. Stumble. Stand up. Have a setback. Keep going, faster. Face a challenge. Out-think it. Hit a wall. Scale it.

The choice is ours to take in feedback, and then let it show us our opportunity. We don't always know where opportunity will take us, but all paths lead to success.

CHAPTER 16

The Win–Win–Win

Money alone sets all the world in motion.

—Publilius Syrus

The entrepreneurial spirit of the Awakened Millionaire is expressed in three words: win–win–win.

When we stay true to our creed, true to our mission, and true to our values, then everyone wins. We win, our customers win, and the community wins.

We win because we have successfully delivered immense value to our customers. Our customers win through the impact our product or service offers them. The community, whether it's local or global, wins by the proliferation of positive actions happening within it.

Just one transaction imbued with the win–win–win spirit generates a ripple effect that can touch hundreds, thousands, and in some cases, millions of lives.

A little-known secret to attracting success in all areas of life is to look for the win–win–win in every relationship.

- I don't want to win but have the other side lose.
- I don't want just a win–win, either, though both sides winning is pretty cool.
- I want to complete the circuit with *everyone* involved winning.

This is far more than what most people do. Let me explain with a story.

For the past 10 years we have lived peacefully in the Hill Country of Texas. We love it here. There is a vacant, two-acre lot beside my home office. The owners of it visit their property once a year and when I see them I try to buy it from them. They refuse. They come back a year later. I offer to buy it again. They refuse. And so it goes. The situation has been acceptable as they haven't built anything on the property in all this time. It's been quiet. All is well.

But recently they sent workers and surveyors out to their land. The writing was on the wall. Construction would begin soon. I was facing a year of noise from the building of their home, and then a lifetime of neighbors. I dreaded it. I was imagining my serenity gone forever.

I knew there had to be a win–win–win *someplace* here. I just couldn't see it. What was I going to do? Where's my win–win–win, I wondered?

Nerissa, my wife, jumped online and found a five-acre tract of land for sale near us. She looked it up to get a sense of the price of land in our area. We were going to use that info to make a last-ditch offer to buy the neighbor's land. But her finding that information led me to come up with a wild idea. I received an idea that I was pretty sure was genius. I thank my intuition for it, as well as my ability to see an opportunity and act on it.

I found the realtor for the five acres and told her, "If you're good at one phone call, I can get you two sales of land."

She was intrigued. I told her the story of the two acres beside me. I told her about the five acres near us. And then I said, "Call the owners of the two acres and tell them I will buy their land for the price of the five acres down the street."

That would be a win–win–win.

This way I would get their land, they would get a much bigger lot for their home, and the realtor would get two sales. Win–win–win.

Yes, I would be paying almost twice what the two acres are worth, but emotionally, that land meant a million dollars of freedom to me. It is *well* worth the investment.

Not everyone would do this, of course. Most would fight to find a way to get the two acres and nudge out the neighbors. That's a single win.

Another person might go for the win of the two acres, and try to help the owners of the acres find the equivalent land. That's a win–win but not one to write home about.

Few would think to include the realtor. They'd use a shadow buyer to somehow cut out the realtor. But that's a win–win, not a win–win–win.

Again, a little-known secret in life is to go for the win–win–win. I do the same thing in my affiliate programs. If I endorse something, then I have used the program and love it so much I am now an affiliate for it (win), I know the creator of the program is making a fair profit from selling it through me (win), and I know the end buyer of it will be happy (win).

Why don't more of us do this?

Most of the time we get lazy and just come from the mindset of taking care of our own needs. But I've found that the true joy in living is in taking care of your needs while you *also* take care of others.

Here's one more story to illustrate my point. Recently I was watching an incredible documentary called *Rock Prophecies*, about this amazing photographer for the rock stars. Robert Knight has photographed the icons of music, from Led Zeppelin, Slash, Jeff Beck, and the Rolling Stones to Stevie Ray Vaughan, Santana, Sick Puppies, and more. Today he looks for the yet-to-be-discovered legends, such as Tyler Dow Bryant. His story is riveting and inspiring.

The photographer typically doesn't sell the negatives to his breathtaking rare photos. He was the only photographer at Stevie Ray Vaughan's last concert, for example, yet he's never released those photos or many others, of many other stars. He's been offered over $3 million for his entire collection, but he will not sell.

But then Robert's mother got Alzheimer's. She had to be put in a constant-care facility. This was going to cost about $9,000 a month. The photographer didn't know what he was going to do but he knew something had to be decided.

Out of apparently nowhere, the sister to Jimi Hendrix contacted Robert. They worked out a win–win–win deal where Robert would sell the negatives of his Jimi Hendrix photos to Jimi Hendrix's sister and the Hendrix foundation, and in exchange he would get enough money to pay his mother's health bills every month. Obviously this is a win–win–win. Robert got the money. The Jimi Hendrix foundation got the rare photos. And Robert's mother is getting the care she needs.

Do you see how this works? What I'm really talking about here is love. Love everyone involved in your negotiation and partnership and you'll naturally attract the win–win–win.

The next time you are faced with a negotiation, a sale, or a relationship issue, ask yourself, "Where's the win–win–win here?" If you assume there is one, then your mind will start looking for it. So turn on your mental radar for the next win–win–win.

The win–win–win spirit embodies the global perspective of the Awakened Millionaire. We act locally, but reach globally. We strive to extend our impact as far as it will reach. We do not look myopically at the actions we take. We do not limit ourselves. We stretch as far as we can.

The win–win–win is a problem solver, in addition to a mindset.

The greatest challenges awakened millionaires come up against are often resolved with the question: What is the win–win–win? If we identify what is commonly known as competition, what is the best way to approach them? We can reach out, join forces, brainstorm, and cooperate. We all offer something unique—we can only grow stronger when we support each other.

Hold an event and get twice as many attendees. Offer a product that offers two unique approaches, and reach twice as many people. Refer customers to the competition when appropriate, and vice versa. We may find that the competition transforms into an invaluable ally. We've seen how feedback leads directly to opportunity.

Awakened Millionaires empowered with the win–win–win expand the reach of opportunity. For example, a company makes organic, sustainable body products and gives a percentage of their profits to rainforest preservation. The company noticed that customers complain frequently that the pumps on their plastic bottles jam and need to be replaced. While they have always used recycled plastic for their packaging, they take this opportunity to redesign their bottles with a plastic-like material made from corn, and add a squeeze top. The squeeze top is far cheaper than the old pump, which more than offsets the cost of using the state of the art corn-based material. Now their bottles don't jam, are biodegradable, and slightly cheaper to produce. Everyone wins, including the environment.

As entrepreneurs, we are always ethical, always generous, always going above and beyond. We are always focused on the good of others —and we know that not only is this the right thing to do, but it nurtures the growth of more wealth and more spiritual enrichment at the same time.

We cannot lose as Awakened Millionaires. We are on a constant quest to expand our reach, knowing that every life touched is a victory.

CHAPTER 17

The Big Idea

Empty pockets never held anyone back. Only empty heads and empty hearts can do that.

—Norman Vincent Peale

The Awakened Millionaire is guided by visions of what we can accomplish through our entrepreneurial might. We understand, through and through, that our profits come second to our mission, that our personal reward is tempered by our communal impact. As we move forward as Awakened Millionaires, we sharpen our mission not only through the growing strength of our passion, but by the emerging shape of our awakened entrepreneurship.

Standing in support behind our efforts is our Big Idea. This is our fundamental reason for our entrepreneurship. This is our understanding of what we offer now, what we're capable of offering, and ultimately what we will offer as our Big Idea comes to fruition.

For many entrepreneurs, their Big Idea is profit. It doesn't mean they are devoid of passion for their customers, but it is not their driving force. They will likely wake up in the morning asking, "How will I make more money today?" As Awakened Millionaires, we wake up asking, "How will I make a bigger impact today?" It is more than virtues. It is more than the creed. There is also an evolved understanding that, in this modern era, our profit is a direct result of our passion to help others. And our Big Idea is the succinct expression of this passion.

This Big Idea is there for our own vision. It is our internal guiding system. It is how we understand our actions, how our intuitions direct our actions, and how we build upon our actions. It is our passion and based on our passion; it grows from our passion. It is, first and foremost, for our own understanding and evolution.

The people we serve see another side of the Big Idea. They see our Big Promise. This is our entrepreneurial mission for all to see. It is what we offer our audience. It is what we guarantee our customers before we ever exchange money. Our Big Promise is a solemn pledge we do not back down from and do not abandon. Instead, we persistently evolve it.

Our Big Idea and our Big Promise are in a persistent spiral upwards. It contains the cycle of feedback as our Big Promise interacts and evolves on the outside and comes back to elevate our Big Idea on the inside. We rely on this feedback loop, this call and response, this cause and effect. We rise as a result.

Our Big Idea is coded in a language intended for us. It does not require translation for others' understanding. But our Big Promise pushes us to articulate our visions beyond our own understanding. We are forced to translate our vision so that others can not only understand, but also respond. That means we don't speak in the language of logic, but in the poignant code of desire and benefit for those we serve.

The Big Promise simply states how our product or service elevates our audience to achieve their one biggest desire. It not only helps people decide whether to stand out from the crowd and join us, but it helps keep us accountable to our community. If our offerings are anchored in a simple, clear, Big Promise, we cannot hide. We are accountable from start to finish. This accountability makes us stronger and bolder as Awakened Millionaires, so we must carefully craft this lynchpin to our efforts.

We cannot fall into the common pit traps of the common entrepreneur. Our Big Promise cannot try to force people to want something they don't already desire. Our Big Promise cannot try to speak to people who are fundamentally not interested.

If we break these cardinal rules, we begin to erode the power of our Big Promise, without our awareness. We rely on its evolution to evolve us. We rely on its feedback to push us. We rely on its truth and stability to rest our mission; a fundamental flaw in its foundation can set us back. We have no time for avoidable setbacks.

If we stay true with our Big Promise, and grow with it as it grows, we have an unshakable foundation to build our enlightened enterprise. Our enlightened enterprise is how we make money. Our enlightened enterprise is one of the ways we express our soulful purpose.

Money + Soul = More Money + More Soul

SECTION TWO

You

CHAPTER 18

Who You Can Become

You can only become truly accomplished at something you love. Don't make money your goal. Instead, pursue the things you love doing, and then do them so well that people can't take their eyes off you.

—Maya Angelou

I don't know where you are today.

I don't know the shape of your personality, the contours of your subconscious, or the design of your life. I don't know if you're happy with who you are, or long for a transformation. I don't know if you feel pride in who you are, or struggle with who you are. Perhaps you have all of this within you.

But I do know who you can become. You can become the embodiment of soul collaborating with money. There is no single, absolute vision of the perfectly actualized Awakened Millionaire. We are people, not robots. But there is a common path laid out for you. A path etched in time, paved with success stories that precede you. It is built on the "Manifesto" and imbued with the "Awakened Millionaire's Creed."

You have now seen where we will walk together. We have shared that space together, you and I. But now, you must traverse that road for yourself and carve out the path that suits your soul, your passion, your purpose, and ultimately, your mission.

Your mission is not yours alone. It is supported by the creed. It is informed by the creed. It is guided by the creed. In your own mission, you will find the greater mission we all share:

You will be dedicated to making a positive impact with your passion, your mission, and your money.

Your business will be driven by the desire to elevate all of us, not just yourself.

Your mission will be an expression of gratitude not only for your own purpose and success, but for the soulful and financial return you receive when you bring your mission to the world.

Your mission will be defined by the win–win–win, always focused on adding value to the world you live in as it rewards you with your own prosperity.

Your mission will be inspired by the overall mission to elevate more people to the path of the Awakened Millionaire, leading by example, and helping others find their own way to realize the formula: soul + money = more soul and more money.

I want to take you there. I want to guide you through what you will look like as the actualized Awakened Millionaire. I want to help you till the soil and plant the seeds.

It will take time.

Awakening your entire relationship with money can take time. Honing your mission into a practical vision will take time. Mastering the awakened path through entrepreneurship will take time. Embrace it.

Yet the Awakened Millionaire can begin to take shape within you now, here, in this moment. The rewards are seen tomorrow.

It only begins when the choice is made. A choice you must make. It won't begin until you make that choice to follow the path of an Awakened Millionaire.

Perhaps you already have. If you haven't, I invite you to do more than just dip a toe in the water. If you've followed me this far and do not feel the slightest burning desire, then perhaps this mission is not for you, or not for you now.

But if there is even a hint of a fire within you, a part of your mind, body, and soul reaching out to experience the adventure of the Awakened Millionaire, then sink one foot in, and then the other.

Begin to walk this path in earnest with me. Let me guide you through your beginning as the Awakened Millionaire.

CHAPTER 19

Decision

Money is usually attracted, not pursued.

—Jim Rohn

Decision

If you will step one foot in, and then the other, you must then lower your center of gravity and dig your heels into the dirt. It is time to make a decision.

For you, as the Awakened Millionaire, are a decisive creature. You do not prolong decisions that must be made. You make your decisions with conviction, for there is power in decision.

While fear holds others back from making certain decisions, you plow through. The fear will not disappear simply because you wish it. Fear, in whatever shape, will be there. But you are not slowed down by fear, and if you are, not for long—for there are decisions to be made, actions to be taken, and abundance to be achieved.

Fear is the Great Feedback. Fear lets you know you're on the right path. If you do not feel that fear, it might mean you are not pushing yourself close enough to your true potential as an Awakened Millionaire.

The transformations before you can be uncomfortable, especially with the screaming of your subconscious that doesn't want to change. Our subconscious minds are quite content where they are; they cherish their control. But ultimately, we must reshape our consciousness to embrace change, embrace fear, and become our cherished ally.

You will make mistakes. You will stumble. You might suffer. You might quickly realize there was a better way—but you are not shaken in these moments. Challenges are opportunities to learn.

There are no bad decisions when made with earnest conviction and full intention. There are only opportunities to learn and grow. We will always do our best to make the best decisions possible, whether through our empowered intuitions or through the moments where careful consideration is called for.

Others become trapped in moments when many options lay in front of them. Others feel the paralysis of the analysis, perpetually wondering whether they will regret their decision once it's made. You do not. You may feel the weight of the decision at hand, but you will not let that weight or any fear stop you from moving forward.

And now you make a weighty decision: Are you ready to set off? Are you ready to transform yourself, bit by bit, day by day, into an Awakened Millionaire?

I would call it your destiny as a soulful person with a desire to usher prosperity into your own life, and the lives of those around you. But I cannot tell you what song your soul is singing right now. Are you an Awakened Millionaire to be? Are you ready to walk the path?

Will you join me?

You Begin

Here we stand, you and me. We stand at a crossroads, a point where the decision is real. You walked with me as we traversed the new landscape of the Awakened Millionaire. You heard the rallying cry, you saw the far-reaching vision, and you felt the urgency, both for us and for those we help.

Now you must decide whether you will join this movement. You must decide whether you are ready and willing to set off on the quest to transform yourself.

The beauty of adventures like this is that you see your own transformation every day. You will notice the changes in your thinking, in your attitude, in your very nature. You will notice how these changes ripple out into your immediate surroundings. You will notice how others stop and notice a new, quiet radiance. You will notice the way money comes to you differently, faster, and with more ease.

But the journey to attaining the true rewards of the Awakened Millionaire will not happen overnight. It will not be a magical transformation. It will not come wrapped with a pretty bow.

You must stay true to your vision, to your passion, to your purpose, and your mission. If you do, you will own a level of achievement that is impossible to describe, as it will be uniquely yours. I cannot promise you what your new life will look like, how much newly awakened money you will make, or how great your impact will be. But I can promise an adventure you will cherish the rest of your life. I can promise you will remember the day you said, "I'm ready," and took your first step.

There will be trials and tribulations. There will be the demands of life that ask for your attention. There will be resistance from others who are wary of change. There will be ingrained parts of your subconscious stubbornly holding on for the dominance they once had, making a racket as they go out kicking and screaming.

You might slip from your convictions. You might grow restless or impatient. You might wander off your path. But you can always find your way back. The adventure of the Awakened Millionaire does not dissipate with time. The benefits do not fade with distance. They will always be there with you, beside you, working to elevate you further.

But if you choose to join us, if you choose to make that commitment to yourself, then stay the course to your greatest ability. Stand strong and firm with your convictions and your actions. If you waver, if you fall off the wagon, do nothing but get back on and carry forward.

We do falter. We do doubt. We do have moments of weakness. We are only human. But Awakened Millionaires do not guilt themselves, chide themselves, or whip themselves into a frenzy. We simply acknowledge when we falter, get back on course, and continue moving towards our awakening.

If you are ready to join me, then let us move forward together. Let us acknowledge the commitment you give to yourself. And let us celebrate, for the journey forward will be unlike any you've known. It will awe you. If you've made your decision to begin this adventure, then anchor it in your soul, acknowledge the opportunity, and let's begin.

CHAPTER 20

Money

All riches have their origin in mind. Wealth is in ideas—not money.
—Robert Collier

Money

There is no more war. Money is no longer your enemy. Any financial struggle you might feel is no longer the fault of an outside force.

You, and only you, have responsibility and you will cherish that responsibility. You are no longer the victim and you will lavish in that freedom. Start now, with a commitment.

Make a commitment to reawaken your relationship with money. Make a quiet pledge to look at money with new eyes. See its simple nature. See its neutral way. See the tool it can be and the soul it can support. You are in control.

Money is not the root of all evil because money is neutral. You are in control. Money is no longer the great destroyer but rather a force of creation of your own design. You are in control. Money cannot corrupt you because it has no power of its own. It only has your power. You are in control. Money cannot harden your heart because you bring love and respect. There is no hardness in love and respect. You are in control.

Money cannot control you, imprison you, or change you. It never could. Only your thoughts about money controlled you. Only your emotions behind money imprisoned you. Only your habits with money chained you.

Those thoughts are changing. You are awakening. You are finding your soulful control. As you move through this moment of reawakening, you wonder, "How could this charade of a war have lasted for so long? How have I lived this falsehood with such precision and commitment?"

Perhaps you feel appalled by the time and energy wasted on such a ridiculous war. Or perhaps it's guilt, shame, shock, or disbelief. Don't fight it. Acknowledge it, respect its presence, and then let it go like a shadow passing with the sun. Let go of any thought or emotion that holds no importance on where you are now: looking forward.

Fortify yourself with the gratitude of knowing you are now free from this war. The fog has been lifted and can never return. You cannot break your shackles, leave the cave, see the light, walk back in the cave, shackle yourself once again, and pretend you never saw the light.

You know what that light is. You know what that freedom is. It is the light and freedom of a life unburdened by a battle with money, an enemy that never existed.

No more cursing your bills, your debts, or your liabilities. There is only gratitude for the lights, the heat, the phone, the car, or the house those bills represent. Write thank you notes on your checks. Send cookies to your debt collector. You will never curse money again, for how do you curse what brings us abundance? It is a ridiculous notion that no longer makes sense to you, the Awakened Millionaire.

When you look at the community around you, you do not see the greed or rot that is money. You see the greed and rot that is a troubled human soul who's lost its way. You do not see wicked control commanding the happiness of helpless souls. You see people ripe for awakening, ready to ascend the hill and see the battlefield where one side fights an enemy that was never there.

If you ever came across a crowd throwing money into the flames, you would not cheer, you would not cry; you would only mourn the opportunity for impact lost to an inherited ignorance our society has lived with for generations.

For you have broken the vicious cycle. The struggle between hate and love has stopped at your feet, no longer permitted a moment of your time. It is not your fate to tangle with this vicious cycle. It never was. You know that now.

You have joined the ranks of the Awakened Millionaires. They may not all know themselves as such. But they know the formula in their bones. And they know the true relationship with money for what it is: potential, power, and prosperity.

You stand with them now, those who neither love money, nor hate money. You stand with those who neither struggle with it, nor fight it. You stand with those who command it, yet respect it. You stand with those who give with it, who transform with it.

And the money will come to you, for it now has a home. It has a safe haven and a nurturing bond. It is allowed to be what it is: neutral. A tool ready for your vision to give it a mission.

Do you lust for it? No. You are an Awakened Millionaire.

Do you cherish it? No. You are an Awakened Millionaire.

Pull out a bill from your purse or wallet. Or pick up a coin from your pocket. Hold it in your hand. It does not breathe. It does not talk. It does not stare at you. It does not feel for you. But it does go where you put it.

Where will you put it?

Just imagine what you can accomplish with your money if it had a mission!

Imagine you had exactly one million dollars in your bank. What would you do with it? How would you use it? How would you live for your mission? How would you make an impact? What cause would you support? What call would you take up? Who would you help?

How would you invest in not just your future, but our future? How would you transform your money into an expression of your passion, purpose, and mission? How would you transform that money into an expression of your soul?

Perhaps you see a clear picture. Perhaps you don't yet. It doesn't matter if it's fuzzy for you now. What matters is that you feel yourself there, feel yourself with the potential energy held in those million dollars, and feel the presence of your passion. On its own, it's just money. It's just paper. With your passion, it's awakened.

Anchor yourself there. Hold that feeling. Hold the taste, the smell, the touch. Feel it with your being. Let it be your guide. For you are not just a millionaire. You are an Awakened Millionaire, and your impact will be felt for years to come.

CHAPTER 21

Obstacle Gold

Money is only a tool. It will take you wherever you wish, but it will not replace you as the driver.

—Ayn Rand

Your Greatest Obstacle Hides Your Greatest Opportunity

Anchor yourself in the power of money, and you make progress. But the greatest obstacle to an empowered relationship with money lies in your head. It's not the thought that money is evil, bad, or corrupting that holds the most power over you. It's the subconscious might of victimhood.

For years, you have felt victimized by money. If you don't have enough money, you are the victim of your job, your bills, or the economy at large. It's money's fault. It's the government's fault. It's the system's fault. It's the bank's fault, or the bill collector's fault, or your spouse's fault.

You have trapped yourself as the powerless victim for years. Not by choice, but by the example of others, by the power we've given money over us, and by the idea that money holds the keys to our personal freedom.

But you are not the victim—you know that now. You are not the victim of money or the government. You are not the victim of your bills, your debts, or your spouse's willful spending.

This is progress. But simply acknowledging this is not enough. You can begin to transform your conscious understanding of this false victimhood, but this won't take you where you must go.

Why?

Because your victim mentality extends beyond your relationship with money. In fact, the victim mentality is so ferocious in its persistence that many people sadly go to their deaths feeling like they have been the victim from start to finish.

Do you ever blame others for your problems in life? Victimhood.

Do you ever complain about the situation you're in? Victimhood.

Do you ever complain about your friends, your family, your neighbors, or even strangers? Victimhood.

To redesign our relationship with money, we must relinquish our victim mentality. While it's not as simple as willing it away, it is easier than you might think. In fact, the solution lies in a critical transformation you make as an Awakened Millionaire: You take responsibility. You replace victimhood with acceptance of your own power.

You are the only one responsible for your life. Never forget it. There is not one single situation where you can justify remaining the victim. Not one, for you are in control.

Yes, life happens. Events happen. Sickness happens. Surprises happen. Sadness happens. Challenges happen, and these events outside of ourselves are not always in our control. But how you choose to respond is.

You control your attitude to whatever life brings you. You control the relationship you have with your struggles. You control what you do next. You control how you move forward and respond. That is responsibility, and there is power in taking responsibility.

Do not relate to responsibility as if it were a burden. See it as a powerful opportunity. For control is one trait that few people ever champion. For many, the thought of having responsibility for every action you take, and every response you have, can be daunting. It can be frightening—it can make us want to hide.

But you, as the Awakened Millionaire, never hide. You don't want to hide. Because in responsibility lies your power, and that power is joyful. The moment you stand firm and champion your responsibility is the moment you are free.

Your subconscious mind, where victimhood has bred and thrived, will fight back. But its claws are weak and trimmed when you take back control. They are no match for the thrill of responsibility.

You are not perfect. . . . You might catch yourself beginning to complain. You might catch yourself beginning to blame others. You might catch yourself assuming you have no power over what happens next. But you will catch yourself. Once you see the light, you cannot unsee it. Responsibility empowers you. You will have more power than you ever realized.

Inspired by this? Good. Run with it. Intimidated by this? No problem. Face your fear and sit with your awakened power. Sit with your power. Acknowledge it. Feel it course through you. It will begin to feel good. It will begin to feel right. You will feel like you've come home.

Welcome home.

Most people are oblivious to how much power they have over their own lives, but you are now aware.

You've found freedom in your responsibility. Take responsibility. Drown your victimhood in your own power. See the complaints, excuses, or blame crumble inwards.

Feel the excitement of a life free of victimhood. Feel the rush of a life where you're in control of what you do next. Feel the love of freedom swirl inside you. Feel the gratitude for what you can now bring to life.

Now collect those feelings into a whirling ball of energy. Let them resonate with your very being and become the embodiment of excitement, the rush, the love and gratitude. Take these emotions and pour them into this power of responsibility and control over your own life.

Your power is now anchored in that excitement. Your power is now anchored in that rush. Your power is now anchored in that love. Your power is now anchored in that gratitude. When you add the fiery power of emotion into an idea, an intention, or a passion, it tends to become a reality.

Anchor your new awareness of power in these emotions that already feel so good and your power will stay with you.

Anchor yourself in the excitement. Anchor yourself in the rush. Anchor yourself in the love. Anchor yourself in the gratitude, and your power will come to life.

Whether it feels like a miracle, magic, or an act of the Divine, the reality is much simpler: you have awakened.

CHAPTER 22

Empty Full

Money never starts an idea. It is always the idea that starts the money.
—Owen Laughlin

Empty Like a Master, Full of Power

Tai Chi masters are awe-inspiring people rife with lessons to share. Tai Chi, often called an internal martial art, is a Taoist art rooted in the creation of energy, fortitude, and power.

The daily practice of Tai Chi masters is not fierce fighting or sparring. Their daily practice is a slow dance as they fill every movement with this internal power.

They empty, so they can be filled with power.

There are videos of masters of this internal martial art launching people across the room with a light push. It's because they have so much stored, potential energy within every fiber of their being, that a slight opening of the spigot produces a torrential downpour of power.

But, while inspiring, that's not the point.

You see, they don't fight with power. They fight with emptiness. You can't even call it fighting. They are simply responding and adapting, matching any force that comes at them with the exact opposite . . . emptiness.

They are the living embodiment of the ancient yin-yang, which simply portrays the dance between extreme opposites. Light and darkness, curled around each other without harsh lines. In the darkness, there is light. In the light, there is darkness. They are one in the same, yet they are opposites.

As an attacker comes at the Tai Chi master with force, the master sidesteps, and meets it with the exact opposite: emptiness.

That attacking force simply trips over its own redirected momentum. This master, filled with so much power and force, has no need to use it.

You, as an Awakened Millionaire, can adapt this ancient art form for your own daily challenges, and the challenges lurking in your own mind.

You spent a lifetime honing subconscious thoughts buried deep within you. Victimhood is only one expression of them. As you move about your day, they will often remain out of our conscious view. But if you look, you will see them.

They are in your habits. They are in your perspectives. Your patterns and judgments. Your instincts. Your emotional responses. While victimhood was a large beast occupying much of your subconscious, it is not the only beast you contend with. Doubts, fears, self-sabotage. . . .

Your doubts are the expressions of your limiting beliefs. Your fears are the expressions of your mental blocks. Your self-sabotage is the expression of your counter-intentions.

They will not simply disappear because you will it, but they don't have power over you if you follow the lessons of the Tai Chi master:

When you feel the creep of victimhood, you don't fight. You empty.

When you feel the creep of self-doubt, you don't fight. You empty.

When you feel the creep of fear, you don't fight. You empty.

When you feel the creep of self-sabotage, you don't fight. You empty.

As you rebuild your relationship with money, your limiting beliefs will poke you, your mental blocks will prod you, and your counter-intentions will push you off balance. As soon as you swear off victimhood for empowerment, you must be ready, because your subconscious mind will rebel.

But, like the Tai Chi master, you don't fight back, you don't push back, you don't hit back. You simply empty. You empty as the Tai Chi master empties when facing an attack:

You match the doubt with understanding. You match the fear with compassion. You match the sabotage with empowerment. You let the doubt fall on deaf ears. You let the fear disintegrate in the love.

You let the sabotage cower in the presence of your power, but never by force.

You don't fight back, push back, or hit back. You empty and keep moving, and as you gain more power, your subconscious demons will lose power. You will move forward.

CHAPTER 23

The Three

O Gold! I still prefer thee unto paper,
Which makes bank credit like a bark of vapour.

—Lord Byron

The Light of Three

Where do you channel this power? Free of victimhood, becoming empowered—now what?

Like the Tai Chi master, internal power is stored as potential energy. The Awakened Millionaire understands this energy is kept until the moments when it's most needed. Your power is fuel, primed and ready to drive the three potent forces backing your Awakened Millionaire journey: passion, purpose, and mission.

Deep love of something or profound desire—passion.

A simple goal all the way to your reason for existence—purpose.

Your calling or vocation is passion and purpose combined—mission.

Where does your passion lie? It lies where your heart is. It lies where you love what you're doing. It lies where you love what you're studying. It lies where you love what you're thinking about. It lies where you love what you're talking about. It's what makes you happy. It's what you would do if you had all the time, money, and freedom in the world.

There is passion behind the Awakened Millionaire. Every action you take is passionate. Every intention you set is passionate. Every dream you concoct is passionate.

Cars, cooking, electronics, ceramics, golf, healing, travel, cats, dogs, lizards, pink flamingos, lawn care, castles, gardening, airplanes—it doesn't matter—for inside every passion is a path for the Awakened Millionaire to walk.

How do you find that path? You let the path find you. You open yourself, empty yourself, and listen to your intuition. You sit still and feel where your mind, heart, and soul wander. You go where you keep returning to.

Where you find sheer joy, you find passion. Where you find excitement, you find passion. Where you find enthusiasm, you find passion.

There is no mission without passion. There is no Awakened Millionaire without passion. It is the work of your soul, the expression of your spirituality, and the embodiment of your true purpose. Your purpose is found where your passion leads.

As you explore your passions, you discover curious gaps. You find places where there is something missing in the expression of your passion. You find a gap in the marketplace. An aspect of your passion unexplored . . . a book waiting to be written. A lack of community around your passion . . . a website. A need or desire for others who are passionate . . . a business. Your passion is there to fill the gap.

Or you find a flaw in the expression of your passion. You find that information is lacking, education is poor, access is difficult, and needs are unmet. You are there with your passion to fix those flaws.

Or you find stagnation. Your passion lacks innovation in the world. Your passion lacks enthusiasm or advocacy. Your passion lacks action. You are there with your passion to pump new life into the mix.

Your purpose is defined by these opportunities. All you have to do is ask, what if? What if there is a better way? What if more people knew about this? What if there is easier access? What if there is a solution missing?

These what-if questions breed a goal for you to follow, a purpose where you place your passion. Follow the what if and you have your business, you have your cause . . . You have your mission.

Combine your passion with the purpose that emerges, and you can be off to make your impact.

You have your business grounded in a mission. You have your efforts grounded in a mission. You have your gifts for the world grounded in a mission.

Channel your passion, find your purpose, and build your mission.

You have arrived equipped as all Awakened Millionaires are equipped . . . with their passion, their purpose, and their mission.

This is the soul of the Awakened Millionaire. This is your soul brought to life.

Now combine it with money. . . .

CHAPTER 24

Money Soul

They deem me mad because I will not sell my days for gold; and I deem them mad because they think my days have a price.

—Kahlil Gibran

The Soul in Money

It's one thing to be free of the fabled money war, free of the victimhood, and live with a healthy relationship with money. It's something entirely different to pour your soul into the money you make, to give it its own purpose and mission.

That's why Awakened Millionaires make money. That's why we start businesses, build organizations, serve customers, and earn money: because your passion, purpose, and mission give your money meaning and direction. This is why you put in the time, effort, and commitment to grow your business. That's why entrepreneurship is at the root of the Awakened Millionaire's path. Sure, you can make money with a good job and low expenses . . . but your passion and purpose are subdued by your time and energy spent on other people's missions.

That's not you. You build a business because your mission demands it.

Yes, the Awakened Millionaire can live with comfort, luxury, and convenience. Taking care of yourself doesn't make you less of a powerful, passionate, and mission-driven person.

But you don't spend it all on yourself. You don't hoard it so it's tucked away from the light. You give it the power of your soulful mission . . . and then you put it to work, boots on the ground, to elevate your mission and make your impact.

Here's what it looks like in real life:

There is a new movement rising in the entrepreneurial ecosystem, the social enterprise. The company, founded on a mission, is fueled by a desire to make a difference and make a profit at the same time. They are driven by the desire to solve a social problem.

The social enterprise is not a nonprofit. They use the framework of for-profit business to elevate and overcome social challenges they believe in. For instance, you have a product or service you sell . . . and part of your profits go directly to solving a social problem.

You have a business that can hire people who need jobs, whether single mothers, the disabled, veterans, or formerly incarcerated people reintegrating into society.

You have a business that unites a nonprofit with other for-profit companies. You build win–win–win relationships they would not have built on their own.

Or you have a business owned not just by you, but by others who also benefit your customers, your employees, or the people you serve. There is no limit to what you can create.

Whatever your passion, there is a way to turn it into profit.

Whatever your purpose, there is a way to support it in a business.

Whatever your mission, there is a way to transform your money into soulful impact.

Don't simply revolutionize your relationship with money—revolutionize your ideas of how money can empower your soul's work. This is the path of the Awakened Millionaire entrepreneur.

CHAPTER 25

Invest in You

If money is your hope for independence you will never have it. The only real security that a man will have in this world is a reserve of knowledge, experience, and ability.

—Henry Ford

Invest

There is no such thing as perfect. There is no such thing as the fully actualized Awakened Millionaire.

You will always grow. You will always continue to grow and if you ever stop growing, you've fallen from the path, and you must get back on. Just as you must breathe to live, you must grow to thrive.

The growth in the Awakened Millionaire highlights a profound understanding you hold: the world is always changing. There is no stagnation in the real world. There is nothing that stays the same way forever. Everything around us gets disrupted and revitalized. Change is the only constant.

You must always change with the world around you. Your mission must adapt to new realities on the ground. And you, as a person, must constantly grow to match the evolving demands you face.

We hear talk of people who don't like change. That is not you. That is not the Awakened Millionaire. You embrace change. You live for growth. Growth is a thrill and change is a challenge. It is your soul stretching outward and forward, always.

But this is not simply about necessity. It's about the love. Build your love for growth and you will experience fulfillment unlike any you've known. For as you commit yourself to evolve, you see the difference between you today, and you yesterday, a week ago, a month ago, a year ago . . . 10 years ago. Witnessing those moments of evolution only empowers you more. You are locked into the constant momentum of evolution and the transformations you experience will be instantly visible, now and long into the future.

It is through growth that our formula comes alive. Without growth, fusing soul and money does nothing. There is no mutual evolution. But with the spirit of growth, the formula breathes deep and reaches wide.

Soul + Money = More Soul + More Money . . . when there is growth to feed it. You are at the center of all of it —your growth dictates where you can go. Without you, there is no passion, there is no purpose, and there is no mission. Without you, your mission does not exist. You fuel the mission that comes to life, and like every type of fuel, it must be replenished. That's why you commit to growth—to feed your soul as your soul feeds your mission.

So you seek new experiences, because that is growth. You take courses and sign up for classes, because that is growth. You find a mentor, because that is faster growth. You rest, so you can keep growing the next day. You meditate to replenish your energy, so you can grow holistically. You have fun . . . for that is the only way any of this will last.

So, ask yourself: How can you improve? If you don't know, find out. How can you reinvent yourself? If you don't know, experiment. How can you discover what's possible? If you don't know, try something new.

You are here because you desire to make an impact. You desire to bring good to the world. You desire to change the world, heal the world, elevate the world, and evolve the world.

You can.

But how much depends on how far you're able to grow and what you're able to become. It depends on whether you commit to ongoing discovery. Devote yourself to a lifestyle of constant growth. Commit yourself to persistent evolution —not because you must, but because it's a thrill . . . and Awakened Millionaires love a thrill.

In your personal life, in your business, at home, in your relationships, with your family . . . you must always champion improvement, reinvention, and discovery.

The lifestyle of constant growth . . . the lifestyle of the Awakened Millionaire.

CHAPTER 26

Your Inner Guide

The best way for a person to have happy thoughts is to count his blessings and not his cash.

—Author Unknown

Your Guide

Money. Soul. Power. Passion. Purpose. Mission. Business. Improvement. Reinvention. Discovery. To many, just one of these is enough to overwhelm them, but not to you, the Awakened Millionaire.

Why?

Because you have your secret weapon. Before rationality, before critical thinking, before planning and scheming, before the juggling act, lies the simple solution that gives you the power to wield all these forces—your intuition.

Your intuition is your guide, your compass, and your decision-maker. It is conviction in action and it requires no special skill. It simply requires you to listen and act.

Your intuition is speaking to you, right now, in this moment. Do you hear it? As you see the peak you strive to reach, as you see the fruits of your passion, and as you imagine the impact your mission will usher forward, your intuition is already working to find the best path to follow.

That's why you don't need maps or plans. There are times to write it down and draw out your options, but only to empower your intuition to guide you. In the light of your intuition, money can be found, soul can be nurtured, power can be wielded, passion can be forged, purpose can be divined, mission can be divined, business can be run, improvement can be natural, reinvention can be effortless, and discovery can be second nature.

Your intuition is your guide, so let it be your guide. Never fall for the idea of the right way. There is no soul, spirit, or adventure in the right way. And there is no need for the right way. Your intuition has taken care of it.

All you must do is embrace all that is in front of you and listen to what to do next—then act. Take one step forward, your intuition knows the next step. Reach a crossroads, your intuition will point your way. Face a challenge, your intuition will guide you safely through.

You do not reach for your intuition. You do not try and activate your intuition. You simply get out of the way. You listen to what your intuition is already telling you. You look at what's in front of you, and the next step will pop out. Your intuition is guiding you.

You sit quietly and allow your mind to wander, and the brilliant idea will be found. Your intuition is supporting you. Embrace your passion as you look out to the world, and your mission will become defined. Your intuition is inspiring you.

If you feel you can't reach your intuition, it's not because it isn't there. Your intuition is alive, well, and active. All you must do is quiet yourself, still yourself, and listen.

Take time to rest, to lie and think, to enrich yourself, to meditate, and to let your mind wander. Your intuition will emerge.

You are not shutting down your logical mind. You are not stopping the process of consideration and examination. You are not blocking out your critical thinking. There are important times for logic, consideration, examination, and critical thinking. But you're letting your intuition make the final decision. Your intuition is taking into account every fiber of your mind, your soul, your thoughts, your emotions, your passions, and your efforts. Your intuition is there with the answer. Listen to it, and when you hear the answer, act.

Act with the conviction of the master improviser. Improvisation is always the expression of your intuition's decision. Improvisation is the movement of your intuition. Improvisation is more than making it up on the spot. Improvisation is articulating what your intuition has decided.

You already know this improvisational spirit. When you have a conversation, you are improvising. When you are exploring a new part of town, you turn left or right based on your improvisational instincts. The more you embrace this trance found in constant improvisation, the more movement you will have and the faster you will go.

Follow your intuition. Follow this pure expression of your soul's intent. Follow the articulation of your mind's cunning. Let go, and simply follow. Your intuition will give you your decision, and your improvisation will put one foot in front of the other.

There is a special confidence that emerges when you follow your intuition, and it emerges when you see the results of your actions. When you see how your intuition has guided you right, you exude a new conviction that only empowers your intuition to sing stronger.

What if you empty, you quiet, and you listen . . . and you hear no voice from your intuition?

Then simply take a step, any step, one foot in front of the other, with no thought of where you're going or how. In that moment, your intuition will kick in not only because it's needed, but because it's free of a restrictive direction. You have no idea of the next step because you do not know where you're going. Embrace that and your intuition will be there.

But it is not simply direction you find within your intuition. You find a bravery you've never known: you can now take on any wild challenge. You can now do what no one else will do. You can now do what others might consider crazy or dangerous.

You find this bravery because you have the conviction of knowing your intuition will guide you through.

There is no challenge your intuition cannot face. It doesn't mean every challenge will be easy. It doesn't mean you will go unscathed. But it does mean that if there is a way through, you will find it—and there is almost always a way through.

Act boldly. Act bravely. Act quickly. Act loudly. Act with intention. Act without hesitation. Take risks. Do what no one else will do.

And follow your intuition, the awakened millionaire's secret weapon, to find the answers you seek.

CHAPTER 27

Where to Begin

We need to make a game out of earning money. There is so much good we can do with money. Without it, we are bound and shackled and our choices become limited.

—Bob Proctor

Begin in the Movement

We have reached the final chapter in this journey, yet the adventure has only begun.

I want to entrust you with a unique mission. A mission that can only succeed in the hands of an Awakened Millionaire. A mission that is both a soulful weight and an immense joy. It is a mission of urgency.

I leave you with the mission to build a movement with me. A movement that is larger than you and larger than me, one that is desperately needed in a world aching for change.

Like most, you opened this book with a thought, and this thought was the deciding factor for whether you kept reading or put it down: "What's in it for me?"

There's nothing wrong with that thought. As you've seen, there's plenty in it for you. There is a transformed relationship with money waiting for you. There is a spiritual power united with financial prosperity waiting for you. There is empowerment and evolution waiting for you. There is the transformation of passion into profit. There is the activation of your intuition as your ultimate guiding force. There is an awakening waiting for you.

These, by themselves, are riches and rewards that can carry you as far as you'll allow them to take you, but, as you've traveled with me to this point, I've revealed levels of suffering and challenges in your own life that perhaps surprised you, and as an evolved soul you can't ignore them.

You discovered the schizophrenic battle taking place in your own head. You discovered the rotting relationship you've had with money. You discovered the immense damage victimhood has wrought on your life. You discovered the inherited beliefs from your family, friends, and society that are holding you back. You discovered the rupture between your soulful purpose and your practical survival.

This world that I paint for you is sickened with lack, victimhood, and suffering at the hands of imaginary enemies, like evil money, wreaking havoc with real consequences.

You came to this book wanting to transform your passion into profit. You came to this book wanting to experience the wealth of a millionaire. You came to this book wanting to awaken and evolve. You came to this book wanting to understand spiritual wealth, and I have planted the seeds within you to take you there, and beyond.

But there is one last seed I want to plant—the seed of the Awakened Millionaire movement.

In this movement, it's no longer "What's in it for me?" In this movement, it's "What's in it for us?"

Take this moment, stand back, and look at yourself where you are now. I have given you the keys to the Awakened Millionaire's power. If you take that power, cherish it, nurture it, and run with it, all the passion, prosperity, and profit you could muster can be yours.

The truth is that I didn't do it for you. I didn't give you this path for your benefit alone—I did it for us. As you learned through shedding yourself of victimhood, taking responsibility is the empowerment that awakens you. With this great responsibility comes great power, but with great power also comes great responsibility.

You now have the power of impact. You hold the power of transformation. You can will the power of evolution. You wield the power of transcendence. You embody the power of awakening.

While I want you to use that power to elevate your own life, to experience your own wealth and spiritual abundance, I did not give it to you to keep to yourself. I gave it to you to spread to others. I gave it to you so you can help heal a world that is sickened by victimhood, has a poisoned relationship with money, and has a disconnect between the spiritual nature of our lives and everyday living. I gave it to you so you can become an agent of change.

Look at the world around you. Stretch your imagination to embrace the realities of the thousands of lives surrounding you right now. There is such profound need for someone with your powers, the powers of the Awakened Millionaire. Your impact can elevate all of us. Your impact must elevate all of us. That is the calling of the Awakened Millionaire.

Why is it that we so often go about our lives turning a blind eye to our own suffering and the suffering of others? Why have you lived so long haunted by the evil specter of money? Why have you remained trapped in the subconscious victimhood without fighting back?

We turn a blind eye because we feel powerless. We feel like we have no control. We feel like nothing we could do could change the realities on the ground. Do you feel that way now?

If you do, I have not accomplished my mission. Because you should be filled with a new sense of power, an awe-inspiring grasp on soulful purpose and mission, and a transformed relationship with money—once an enemy, now an ally.

And more than anything else, you should have a new set of eyes, in full light, seeing the reality in front of you and not just the shadows dancing on the walls.

Let me take it farther. Imagine for a moment that you had the magical ability to see, experience, and soak in the lives of everyone in your small town or big city. Imagine moving through their everyday lives. Imagine witnessing the fights about money, the stress on their faces, and the overwhelming feeling of being trapped. Imagine how their everyday lives are wrapped in the victimhood experience, radiating with their every step. See this money struggle, life stress, victimhood, and caged conflict as an energetic aura surrounding them. It is with them everywhere they go.

Imagine that this aura leaves a thick film everywhere they go. Everyone is painting everywhere they go with this victimhood, this stress, this struggle, and this silent conflict with money.

This little imaginary adventure you just went on is strikingly close to reality, and you were one of those people. The problem is that we think of our lives as if we were in our own autonomous bubbles. What we feel, think, see, and do is ours. It affects us. Yes, it affects our friends, family, and loved ones as well. But its concentrated impact is on us.

This is an illusion. It is a myopic, self-centered way of looking at ourselves. It's not even close to reality. We are such powerful beings by nature that we are indeed spreading everything that we feel, think, and see everywhere we go. We have been spreading our victimhood. We have been spreading our struggle. We have been spreading our everyday stresses. We don't mean to, but we do.

The evil we face is not money; you know that now. The real evil we face is the pervasive suffering we've tainted our entire surroundings with.

There is hope. You are the hope. We, as Awakened Millionaires, are the hope.

I want you to fulfill your role as that hope . . . and I want to paint one last picture.

I want you to imagine that you have become the Awakened Millionaire. I want you to imagine that you're reborn with the power of passion, purpose, and mission. I want you to imagine that you radiate this power from every fiber of your being. I want you to imagine that this power is more contagious than any suffering you once held.

What would happen if you walked through your life, through your community and the world around you, spreading this power of the Awakened Millionaire?

What transformations would we all experience? If you began making money awakened with soul and mission, what impact could you really have? How many lives could you transform?

But it goes deeper than that.

How many people could you help awaken? How many people could you show the true nature of empowerment and responsibility? How many people could you lift up to join you as Awakened Millionaires . . . not by preaching or proselytizing, but by the simple impact of your actions? What kind of force for good are you capable of becoming?

I say you can become a force of untold magnitude, and now that you've had the smallest taste of this power, I say that you have a responsibility to share it, transform with it, and spread prosperity with it. That is the calling of the Awakened Millionaire. That is the greater mission that coexists with your own personal mission. That is the movement that is growing and that I champion here today.

I want you to be prosperous. I want you to have all the money you could ever want. I want you to make that money with the power of your passion and soul. I want you to experience whatever adventure or luxury you choose. I want you to enjoy, through and through, the freedom this prosperity can offer you.

But I want you to ask, "What's in it for us?"

I want you to become a leader who is dedicated to eradicating this evil of suffering. I want you to live by the "Awakened Millionaire's Creed" so you can make the impact only an Awakened Millionaire can make.

I want you to join me, not just in soulful prosperity, but in profound impact. My friend, I am here waiting for you. Will you join me? It's your move.

EPILOGUE

You are walking in a forest of tall evergreens. Nettles crunch softly under your footsteps. You hear ghostly cracks behind you, like thunder or gunshot—a frenetic flurry of notes from a tragic opera.

You are at peace.

Moments ago, you were racked with the guilt of desertion and rattled with the fear of the enemy. Yet it feels distant. You don't know why. You don't need to know why.

The mud caked on your face cracks apart as you curl a quiet smile. It feels like years have passed since you last smiled. You keep walking.

You brush your callused hands against the corrugated trees. You feel the fog nipping at your heels. There is a softness in your walk.

In the distance, a crisp light breaks through the forest's canopy. You see a clearing in the trees, and as you reach the tree line, you notice the fog cowering as it recedes into the forest.

In front of you, a group of kind faces greet you. But it's the smell of their clean clothes that is more striking. The smell of clean clothes—a smell forgotten by the battle-hardened. It's intoxicating.

The group folds around you. They reach out their hands to greet you, their calluses barely a hint of what they surely once were.

"Welcome," says one.

"Welcome home," says another.

A woman steps forward. "We've been waiting for you. There's so much waiting for you."

And in that moment, clarity strikes.

"I know," you say. You pause for a long moment, disbelief for the words you're about to utter: "There's something I must do first."

You look down and softly rub your thumb against your calluses. The sun feels so welcoming to the backs of your hands. The smell of clean clothes is so intoxicating. And sleep. . . .

You take a deep breath. You smile compassionately, knowingly. You turn around and walk back towards the fog, the ghostly cracks waiting for you.

The others who fought by your side are still in there, still throwing futility and bullets against a row of butchered trees. They don't know why they're fighting, but they fight hard and fight on.

They are good people. You must bring them back home. The fog engulfs you and your knowing smile.

You'll be back.

BONUS SECTION

THE AWAKENED MILLIONAIRE'S PRAYER

(Based on *The Secret Prayer* by Joe Vitale)

Thank you. Thank you for all I see and do not see that supports me. Thank you for my life, being, mind, soul, and intention to do good in the world. Thank you for my place to live, for my income, for my ideas and energy and willingness to succeed. Thank you for the planet that sustains life in and around me. Thank you for my relatives and ancestors who contributed to all that is good in me. I am grateful beyond words. I feel this gratitude deep in my being, and I give thanks for all that has made up me.

I request money and consciousness so I can contribute my passion to the world in a way that makes profit while making a difference. I request that I be shown the ways to achieve my noble goals and ask for the clarity and willingness to act on them. I ask that my health and wealth not only help me and my family and friends, but the community and the world. I ask for this or something better to enter my life now and transform all of us for the highest good of all.

I promise to act on the ideas and opportunities that come to me, paying attention to my inspiration and intuition as well as my intellect, knowing that doing my part in the world will help cocreate the results I want to see for myself and others. I will listen and act, reflect and proceed, knowing that each step along the way is the journey as well as the destination.

As an Awakened Millionaire, I uphold the ideals that create a working world based on love and peace and passion.

So be it. So it is. Thank you. Amen.

THE ABUNDANCE MANIFESTO 10 PRINCIPLES

In 1962, Ben Sweetland wrote, "The world is full of abundance and opportunity, but far too many people come to the fountain of life with a sieve instead of a tank car . . . a teaspoon instead of a steam shovel. They expect little and as a result they get little."

How about you? What vessel are you filling at the fountain of life?

Whatever it is, I hope it's big and worthy of all that you are—because you deserve it. Yet for many people, this issue of deservingness is a point of confusion. They don't understand that it's their *birthright* to have everything life has to offer.

You deserved it the day you were born.

Given this, what is it that prevents people from accessing the abundance that is rightfully theirs?

I believe the answer is found in these 10 principles, which I first wrote about in my blog prior to the release of my audio program, *The Abundance Paradigm: Moving from the Law of Attraction to the Law of Creation.* They're my observations about how you can attract personal and planetary wealth—and how I went from homeless to multimillionaire.

Of course, abundance is more than money, so these ideas are more sweeping than you may at first realize.

Abundance is about living in a world of possibilities—and acting quickly on the ones that divinely inspire you. There's only one thing that can stop you . . . your own mind. Fortunately, you can change that.

With this little bonus report, *The Abundance Manifesto*, you can expand your own capacity to receive all the good things in life—and throw away that teaspoon.

Once and for all.

Introduction

The 10 Principles of Abundance

Abundance is not something we acquire. It is something we tune into.
—Wayne Dyer

Everyone can use more abundance in some area of life, but, more often than not, recognizing it in the first place is really the issue.

Life is abundant, clear and simple.

If you're not in it, or feeling it, it's because you've temporarily blocked your awareness of it.

That's what this book is about—bringing awareness to the ways we block abundance, and the ways we can access it.

There are 10 principles, each laid out in its own chapter, along with an exercise to expand that chapter's concept. I recommend reading the book completely through once, then going back and rereading it one chapter at a time. Make that principle your day's focus. When you're done, start over and continue this process for at least 30 days.

Eventually, abundance will permeate every cell in your body, becoming natural and normal to you.

You'll discover abundance was here for you all along. Your search is over.

Principle 1

Thou Shall See the Alternative Reality

When you are grateful, fear disappears and abundance appears.
—Anthony Robbins

In every moment you have a choice. You can see the limitation before you, or you can see the abundance before you.

Life is an optical illusion. What you see depends on your mindset.

Your mindset depends on your programming. Because most of us are programmed by the negative-seeking media, as well as our education, parents, and all else around us, most of us are seeing the scarcity reality.

Yet an abundance reality also exists.

In other words, are you seeing an old woman or a young woman in the famous art from the late 1800s? It depends on your focus. Relax your view and you can see both ladies exist.

The same is true for reality.

It's time to move from seeing the world as scarcity- and fear-based to the world that also exists that is abundance- and love-based. You have a choice. Allow your eyes to see the new world.

Exercise

Think of something in your past that troubled you at the time, perhaps a relationship that ended, or a job you left—then ask the following questions: (Please note that wherever I've used the word *it*, you can substitute the word *him* or *her* if that's more appropriate.)

- How did you see it then and what was your story about it?
- What made it feel negative?
- Now think about where you are today. When you look back, what positive gift or benefit did you receive as a result of having that?
- What purpose did it serve or role did it fill at the time?
- What positive gift or benefit are you enjoying now because of it, or because of what you learned?

Now think of something troubling you right now in your life and consider the same questions.

- How do you see it and what is your story about it?
- What makes it feel negative?
- What positive gift or benefit are you receiving as a result of having it?
- What purpose is it serving or role is it filling?
- Looking into the future, how could this be of benefit to you?

They say hindsight is 20/20 because we can see the perfection of something at a distance. But we don't have to wait to see the gifts. We have a choice to see the abundance now.

Principle 2

Thou Shall Worship Passion

> *I never went into business to make money—but I have found that, if I have fun, the money will come.*
>
> —Sir Richard Branson

The scarcity-based view of the world worships money.

The abundance view worships passion.

When you focus on doing what you are passionate about, money will follow (as long as you practice the other nine secrets in *The Abundance Manifesto*). Passion refers to the joy you get from doing something you care about and feel inspired to do.

Passion is the energy of Divine inspiration living through you.

When you express passion, you express love. When you live from love, you are experiencing the abundant essence of the Universe.

Take your eyes off money and put them on following your bliss—on following your life calling or mission.

This is the direct road to abundance.

Exercise

Think of something you like to do that:

a. When you imagine yourself doing it, you can't help smiling.

b. You haven't taken the time to do in a while (or at all). Ideally, make it something very simple and accessible, such as

- A walk by yourself or with a loved one.
- Playing with your children or animals.
- Puttering in the garden or knitting.
- Learning and practicing a new language or musical instrument.
- Listening to music.

Spend the next five minutes imagining you are doing this activity, taking into account the following:

- What sights do you see? Who's there with you?
- What sounds do you hear? Laughing? Talking?
- Where are you? In the park? In a class? At home?
- Can you touch it? How does it feel in your hands or against your body?
- What positive emotions are you feeling? Peaceful? Content? Excited?

Write down a time to actually do this activity with the intention to keep your promise, either today or this week. If someone is involved with you in the activity, talk to them and share your vision, along with any details about how you'd love it to be. Agree on the day and time together.

There's always something we can do today towards inviting more passion and joy in our life, even if it's only a small step. It's the direction that matters.

Principle 3

Thou Shall Give 10 Percent of All Income

Tithing gives you the greatest return on your investment.
—Sir John Marks Templeton

The ancient principle of tithing asks you to give 10 percent of what you receive as a gift to wherever you received inspiration.

Giving leads to receiving.

Giving is the nature of the Universe.

When you give, you slip into the flow of life. Giving is the very essence of abundance. Give wherever you receive spiritual or inspirational nourishment.

Skipping this secret means you still believe in scarcity, else you would give.

Giving is a concrete statement of abundance.

Exercise

1. Think of an area of your life where you feel you have enough resources. It can be tangible or intangible, such as money, time, or something else you value. Whatever it is, starting with today and for the next 30 days, give some of it away anonymously.
2. Write down how much money you received this month—your total income. How much is 10 percent of that? Then, if you're ready, give that amount today to a place where you receive spiritual sustenance. If 10 percent feels like too much, decide what percentage you can give and do that.

When I first learned this principle, I was afraid to give my money, so I started with something where I felt I had enough to give away—books.

One thing led to another, and once I saw the truth of tithing, I began to give my money. It not only brought abundant increase to me financially, but to every area of my life.

Tithing leverages and multiplies what you already have.

Principle 4

Thou Shall Keep a Clear Mind

There is a lie that acts like a virus within the mind of humanity. And that lie is, "There's not enough good to go around. There's lack and there's limitation and there's just not enough." The truth is that there's more than enough good to go around. There's more than enough creative ideas. There is more than enough power. There is more than enough love. There's more than enough joy. All of this begins to come through a mind that is aware of its own infinite nature. There is enough for everyone. If you believe it, if you can see it, if you act from it, it will show up for you. That's the truth.

—Michael Beckwith

Clarity of mind leads to pure abundance.

Beliefs about not enough of anything are from scarcity, not abundance. Beliefs that money is bad or there isn't enough for all trigger self-sabotaging actions and self-fulfilling prophecies.

A clear mind is achieved through these 10 principles, as well as by deprogramming your mind from the history of conflict and shortage.

A clear mind is no longer a victim but a cocreator. No longer reactionary but now responsive. No longer lost but clear.

Exercise

Most people associate money with abundance, so we'll use it as an example for the purpose of this exercise. However, don't stop with money—do it for other areas in your life where you'd like to see an increase.

Write down how much income you received this month.

Now double that amount and write that down.

Ask yourself, "Can I see myself creating or receiving this?"

If the answer is yes, double it again and ask the same question. Keep going until the answer is no.

This is where limiting beliefs begin to unveil themselves, things like—"I'm on a salary, I can't make more. That's not realistic. Money doesn't grow on trees. That's too much. That would be too hard. This economy won't let me. There's no way."

Jot down your answers. Awareness starts the process of change.

None of these are facts—they're beliefs in scarcity. All are limiting negative beliefs. Sometimes releasing them is as easy as saying, "Do I really believe that's not possible? Do I really believe it's not possible to make more money?" When you question your beliefs, you loosen their hold, and then you can receive even more.

Principle 5

Thou Shall Choose the Higher Ground in Every Decision

Life in abundance comes only through great love.

—Elbert Hubbard

The ego resists love and forgiveness.

It is an illusion self-created and self-maintained. It causes broken homes and broken dreams.

In every decision, there is a choice: Come from love or come from ego. Most come from the latter. The higher ground is to choose love.

When the choice exists, ask, "What is the more loving decision here?"

Choose love.

Exercise

Close your eyes and imagine a circle of your loved ones gathered around you. Feel the love they have for you and the love you have for them. Now expand that feeling as much as you can. From that space of love, think of a situation you'd like to change for better in your life. While you're surrounded in feelings of love, explain to this gathering what you'd like to be different for yourself. Tell them everything you've done or tried so far, and any mistakes you feel you've made, all the while allowing them to continue loving you. Bask mentally in their unconditional love.

Enveloped in love, consider the issue again and ask yourself, "What action could I take towards solving this now?" Write down any answers you receive.

Love is the gateway of abundance, and not forgiving acts as a block. We can release any blocked energy through forgiveness. When you forgive yourself for any perceived wrongdoing or wrong thinking, you can expand your life and get the flow going. That's when things open up in any and all areas, whether it's romance, health, physical well-being, or finances. So ask yourself, "Where in my life am I still holding on to a grudge against myself or another person?"

Principle 6

Thou Shall Implement Divine Inspiration

As fast as each opportunity presents itself, use it! No matter how tiny an opportunity it may be, use it!

—Robert Collier

Abundance comes to those who act on the gifts given to them from Divine inspiration.

An idea isn't a random event. It is an unexpected delivery from an abundant universe. Not acting on the idea is a refusal of a gift. Acting on it is an affirmation of trust.

Those who implement Divine inspiration tend to profit from their actions. This benefits all.

This is abundance.

Exercise

Find a quiet time when you can spend an hour alone to think about what you really want. One way to do this is to think of a situation you don't want in your life, and then write down the ideal outcome.

State the ideal as an intention, declaring it both in written and verbal form.

Next, *Nevillize* your goal (I wrote about this in *The Attractor Factor*.) Visualize yourself already having your desire. See it as if it's already come to pass. It's not in the future; it's now. You are healed and the situation is healed.

Now it's time to let go and release it. This is the point of trust and faith.

Over the next week, take immediate action on any intuitions or ideas that come to you—because they will. It could be something as simple as getting on the computer to do some research around your goal.

Having faith means to relax . . . and know your desire is on its way. Just as importantly, know that you'll be okay in the meantime. This state of relaxed energy puts you in a space of receptiveness to hear the quiet whisperings of Divine inspiration.

Principle 7

Thou Shall Spend, Invest, and Save Responsibly

Many folks think they aren't good at earning money,
when what they don't know is how to use it.
                                                —Frank A. Clark

Abundance is the reality of balance and sufficiency.

As long as you spend, invest, and save in a balanced way, all is well. This needs coupled with the principle of giving (Principle 3), which can be considered a form of investing, but the point remains: whatever you receive monetarily should be split within these areas.

Doing so maintains the abundant life.

Exercise

Draw a circle on a piece of paper. This represents your total income now.

Assign a percentage to various parts of how you currently allocate your dollars. For example, 10 percent to savings, 10 percent to tithing, 30 percent to taxes, 5 percent to debts, 40 percent to living expenses, and 5 percent to spend.

Fill in these percentages on your pie chart.

Notice what's out of balance, or what's missing. For example, maybe you're not tithing or saving and would like to.

Next, draw another circle and create it as you'd like it to be, then post it some place you can see it regularly.

You can also do a pie chart for just one aspect. For example, savings could be split into percentages for investing, for long term and short term, or for particular items you're putting money away for, such as a vacation, Christmas, or a wedding.

Working with percentages offers a way to manage your money easily no matter the amount of income. You'll feel more powerful with the money you have, and as your income grows you'll know what you're going to do with it. Financial security and peace is a part of all abundance.

Principle 8

Thou Shall See Behind Each Challenge

Expect your every need to be met. Expect the answer to every problem, expect abundance on every level.

—Eileen Caddy

Problems are opportunities in disguise. Undress them to see the solution.

Inside every challenge is the resolution to that challenge.

A scarcity mind sees the problem; the abundant mind sees the product, or service, or solution.

You must relax the focus from fire-alarm concern to trusting, heartfelt expectation.

Exercise

Imagine you're an inventor (or an *imagineer*, as they call them at Disney), and that you need to come up with an idea for an invention to compete in a contest.

To begin, you might ask the following questions:

What does not work as well as you would like it to work?
What problem, issue, or dilemma would you like solved?
If you could make life easier, what would you invent?

Next, you'd make a list of alternatives or possibilities, along with any pros and cons, then begin to visualize what form your invention might take and what materials would be needed.

These are just some of the questions inventors ask themselves, but essentially, it all starts with a problem of some sort.

The same process can be applied in solving a personal issue, so, this time, ask the questions about your own life.

Inventors are naturally curious human beings, always sniffing around for a problem to solve—and a problem doesn't have to be bad. For example, at Disney, they're continually trying to come up with an idea for another thrilling ride experience. Problems can be fun when you explore them proactively this way. That's abundance thinking.

Principle 9

Thou Shall Experience the Miracle of Now

One of the most dynamic and significant changes you can make in your life is to make the commitment to drop all negative references to your past, to begin living now.

—Richard Carlson

In this moment, all is well.

This moment is abundance. This moment is the miracle.

Not seeing the miracle of the moment means the ego is limiting the view. Coming from fear is not coming from faith.

When in this moment, where abundance lives and breathes, seeing the next action and next inspiration is a breeze. It's right there.

Exercise

Look around the room you're in and find something you feel grateful for. It can be anything—the chair you're sitting on, a refrigerator, the glass you're drinking from, or the water in the glass.

Make a list of all the things you appreciate about that thing, including the people who made it for you to enjoy. Be creative and reflect on as many aspects as you can.

- What does that object provide you with?
- What comfort do you get out of having it?
- What is it good for?
- What pleases you about it?

Abundance is as close as gratitude because true gratitude always puts you right here, right now—and where else could abundance possibly exist? It's that simple.

Principle 10

Thou Shall Help Others

You can have everything you want in life if you just help enough people get what they want in life.

—Zig Ziglar

Helping others expands your worldview to include the rest of the planet.

It also expands your energy to move it from ego to spirit.

Helping family, friends, community, and the world increases abundance for all. The more you extend a hand to others, the more you feel abundance as a reality for you.

Helping others helps you.

Exercise

Write down something you'd love to do if you had the means to do it.

As an example, let's say you'd like to travel the world and have more fun.

Now imagine you're an entrepreneur looking for a way to not only do both of those, but also create a business that makes money and helps your community.

- You could start a travel agency and sponsor fun tours.
- You could travel around and host sporting events.

Taking what you wrote for yourself, see how many ideas you can come up with around that idea to satisfy your desire—while helping others at the same time.

Relationships, money, all the things we want in life, are going to come through other people. So you've got to make a contribution, and there isn't any way around this. In fact, the more contributions you make while doing what you love, the more you can profit. Think abundance for all.

CONVERSATIONS WITH AWAKENED MILLIONAIRES

(Excerpts from *Hypnotic Gold* interviews by Joe Vitale, www.HypnoticGold.com)

Paul Zane Pilzer served as an economic advisor to two U.S. presidents, and is world-renowned as a leading predictor of economic catalyst and trends. He is author of five best-selling books including *Unlimited Wealth*, *The Next Trillion*, and *The Wellness Revolution*. His books are published in 24 languages. Pilzer started several entrepreneurial businesses, earning his *first $1 million* before age 26, and his *first $10 million* before age 30.

"I believe I am a scientist, as close as an economist can be to a scientist, and I'm realistic. Because, I've certainly called on things that were going to be negative as I did in the savings and loan crisis, which I was one of the first people to write a book about, and predict it was coming in the early 1980s. On the general economy, I'm optimistic and it really comes from fundamental science. I mean all of wealth, if we define it, is based on the physical things we like from housing, food, transportation, cars. All the items we have we might call our wealth.

"Traditional economics is about scarcity. If you remember your first year's economics class, if you went to college or high school and studied economics, the first line is 'Economics is the study of scarcity.' There's a limited supply out there, the old economists say or many economists today say, on land, minerals, and wealth, and fresh water, and oil, and how we rob from Peter and give to Paul. I always liked that analogy. But, really how we take the wealth from one country and give it to another, or take from one have and give it—have not and give it to have, that's economics. And whether you call it communism, capitalism, socialism, or any other ism, the study of economics is really the study of scarcity.

"This bothered me so much that I should probably explain why. My parents, Eastern European immigrants, struggled very hard and they tried to make sense of everything they saw in the United States, and really never could make sense [of it]. My father worked all his life, six days a week, 12 hours a day, and never made, you know, he never made a great living for his family from his standpoint but, of course, never accumulated any kind of wealth that he could stop working until the day he passed away.

"He sent me off to school and then I later went to Wharton Business School to study economics to be an economist. Why? Because the people I love the most, starting with my father, that's the answer they wanted. How do you get wealthy? How do we all get rich? When I got to Wharton I said, "This isn't about how we all get rich, this is how we take from someone else and get rich," because the study of economics is the study of scarcity.

"Anyway, I looked around in my immigrant background starting in the 1950s in United States. Every time I saw vacant land being torn down, you know they took wasteland and built huge housing developments all over Long Island and Westchester, when I was growing up. I was thinking, "No one lived there before; they didn't kick anyone out of their houses." We moved from a little tenement to a nice house in Long Island and so did all my relatives, and so did everyone. I could see all this wealth being created in United States without taking from someone else.

"Then of course, I started running the numbers and realizing that economics is wrong. The foundation of economics—that it's a study of scarcity—is wrong. We should be studying business theories that explain what really is happening. How we're getting more, and more, and more, and more wealthy as a society every year and more and more people are sharing this wealth. That's why I had to develop, originally in the book *Unlimited Wealth*, 15 years ago—well, 17 years ago, a new theory of economics based on abundance, based on the ability of technology to give us abundant wealth without any limit.

"So back to it, I'm not really an optimist, I'm a realist. Because all of wealth, and this is an essential equation running through all my books, wealth is the product of physical resources times technology. $W = P$ (physical resources) times T (technology). $W = P$ times T. It's not how much farmland you have, even though the history of the world for 5,000 years is how to kill the people next door and take their farmland. It's how many—how much—food per acre you produce.

"In the United States, in one example, we took the farmland productivity per acre up 100 times from 1930 to 1980. Or, put it another way, we went from 30 million farmers in 1930 barely feeding 100 million people, to 300 million farmers in 1980. It's much less now, feeding over 300 million people and there's 40 to 50 percent more food. *Wealth equals physical resources times technology.* So, it's not how much farmland you have for food, its farmland times technology, meaning yield per acre."

Randy Gage is a prosperity guru and the author of numerous bestselling books, including *Risky is the New Safe*.

"We live in the greatest time in human history. There has never been a better time to create success. There has never been a greater time to create wealth. There has never been a greater time to go from broke to multimillionaire or multibillionaire in the shortest amount of time than right now, but millions of people don't know that cause they're buying into the bullshit. You know, they're buying into the—they're watching the news, they're reading the news, oh, did you hear the latest job report, what about inflation?

"Understand, your prosperity has nothing to do with your job, your boss, the economy, any of that stuff. Those things are all factors, but your prosperity is created by how you respond to all of those factors and why I wrote *Risky is the New Safe*. I want people to really get that, forget the gloom and doom. We live in the greatest time—if you could get in that DeLorean with Michael J. Fox and you got to pick a date to go to, this is where you'd want to go.

"When you look at mobile, mobile apps, the Cloud, social media, artificial intelligence, cloning, biogenetic engineering, what's going to happen in the next 10 to 15 years is more than what happened in the last couple thousand. There will be such opportunity, yes; it'll be challenging, yes; there's going to be people nervous, anxious, upset—I get all that. But every one of those challenges has a corresponding opportunity and this is the moment that you want to be alive, right here, right now."

Bruce Muzik is an internationally acclaimed speaker, author, and an expert on how to use the human mind to achieve success effortlessly. His philosophy blends leading edge physics with practical spirituality, providing real-world success for his students around the globe.

"Maybe the first thing to do is to distinguish wealth from money and I think the easiest way to do that would be with a metaphor. I'd like you to imagine that money is like butterflies. And most people go through life trying to catch butterflies. They go through life trying to make money and they've got a butterfly net and they go through life trying to catch the butterflies and at the end of the day the butterflies fly away and they've got what they got and they have to come back the next morning. But after a while other butterfly catchers have caught on to the fact that there are a lot of butterflies to be caught in this particular area and they come in with bigger nets and very often outperform you and you go home empty-handed without much money left, or without many butterflies having been caught that day. What ends up happening is that the butterfly catchers have to come back every day, chasing butterflies. They have to get bigger nets. They have to keep on finding new, improved ways to catch their butterflies.

"However, wealthy people don't go around chasing butterflies, Joe. What they do is they build a garden and they attract butterflies into the garden. And what wealthy people know is that at the end of the day the butterflies disappear from their garden, but they know they'll be back the next day because they've tended to a garden that attracts butterflies. So, I'm going to use the garden as a metaphor for wealth and the butterflies as a metaphor for money. What most people are doing is that they are running through life going, "I want to become a millionaire. I want to make lots of money." And they go out there chasing butterflies trying to make money without first having grown a garden, or built a foundation of wealth. So I will use that as kind of a metaphor to introduce this concept and let's talk practically then about what wealth is.

"So, the way Roger Hamilton, my mentor, defines this is that wealth is the intangible things that are unique to you. Your wealth is your network. It's your resources. It's your skill sets. And one of my favorites is it's your track records. It's these intangible—it's a mindset as well—it's the intangible things that you can't see. When wealthy people lose all their money they tend to find that money comes back to them over and over again. They tend to make their money back again."

Rabbi Daniel Lapin is the best-selling author of *Thou Shall Prosper*. *Newsweek* once called him one of America's most influential rabbis. He has presented before Boeing, Microsoft, and Nordstrom, as well as the U.S. Army.

"Now you want to build money channels. What you really would like is for pipes to be drilled through that barrier so money can flow through it to you. That's what we'd all like. The trouble is that you cannot force anyone on the outside to drill money channels through the barrier to you so as money can flow through. And so you can do the only thing you can do, which is drill those holes from your end.

"How do you do that?

"By pushing money out from you. And once those channels have been created by you pushing money out—while those channels still exist and money can still flow in—the surest way to create those channels is by giving money away.

"And additionally when you think about it almost nothing produces the same amount of social connectedness as giving money away. That's one of the reasons that the smallest town in America has a Rotary Club and as you get to bigger towns there's all kinds of organizations— the theater and the orchestra have a charity. What are all these things for? You know, when you get right down to it, is this all because everybody really desperately wants there to be an orchestra in Wichita? You know probably some people do, but for a whole lot of other people being on the board of the orchestra is a way of meeting other human beings. Because people recognize that when you are willing to give money away you make connections and that's the key thing. That's why it is.

"So again, whether you accept it from the Bible as I do, it is just darn good advice for human beings to give away more than 10 percent of their income. The way I look at it, is God is terrific. He lets me work on a 90 percent commission. Ten percent doesn't even belong to me. Here's the beauty of it. When I give it away I'm helping myself more than I'm helping anybody else."

Bill Bartmann created seven successful businesses in seven different industries, including a $3.5 billion, international company with 3,900 employees that he started from his kitchen table with a $13,000 loan. He's been named National Entrepreneur of the Year by NASDAC, *USA Today*, Merrill Lynch, and the Kaufmann Foundation. *Inc.* magazine cited his companies as being among the 500 fastest growing companies in the United States four years in a row. He has been awarded a permanent place in the Smithsonian Institute's Museum of American History and awarded the American Academy of Achievements Golden Plate Award as one of the outstanding achievers of the twenty-first century. Yet, he was once homeless.

"There is an itty, bitty drill that they can do and all it takes is a piece of paper and ballpoint pen. So this isn't high tech or exotic.

"If they were to take just a sheet of paper—and I'll talk slow and let them run to get one right now—and just draw a line down the center of a piece of paper and on the left hand side write the word, "Failure." Underneath that word failure, write down every time that you've screwed up. Every time they've made a mistake, every time they were in the wrong place at the wrong time, everything they wished hadn't happened. I'm not trying to make people feel bad or drag them back to old memories and rip open a scab off an old wound. I just want them to list the thing that they think was a really bad thing that happened in their life. And spend a few minutes doing that and people, trust me, they will drudge up a whole bunch of stuff real quick.

"Then I ask them on the other side of that line write the word, "Success." Write down all the times you've gotten it right. If failing is screwing up, getting it wrong, then every time you got it right isn't a fault, it is a positive. So list all the times you got it right, all the times you made somebody happy, all the times you made somebody proud, all the times you made yourself proud.

"If a teacher ever patted you on the head, or your mom put your report card on the refrigerator, if you ever caught the winning touchdown, if you ever sold more cookies than somebody else. I'm not talking about coming up with the cure for cancer or winning the Nobel Prize, I'm just talking about times you got it right. What will happen every time—and I've done this now thousands and thousands of times—every single time, without exception everyone I've ever done this for has had more items over on the right-hand side than they have on the left-hand side.

"But we're not done. Now, I go, 'That is a great observation. Look, you have more successes than you've got failures. Shouldn't that say something about you?' And of course it does.

"Then I say, 'Let's do something else. Let's go back and look at those failures. How many of those have you overcome? How many of those have you gone through, how many of those have you survived, how many of those really aren't an impediment any more? For all of those, move them over to your success side.'

"Because having suffered through, and in your case being homeless, that is a strength. That is not a negative. You have done something that not everybody can do and that makes you better than some other people. Not better in that your stuff doesn't stink, Joe, but better in that we have suffered through something. And when you can move your failures over to your success side and then finally see yourself maybe clearly for the first time, who you really are, that is powerful.

"The facts are the facts; we can't change them. But it is how we see the facts that change us. So when we look at a negative as a negative, we get all woe is me, I screwed up and I'm not very smart and doggone it. But if we look back at that thing and say, 'Hey, I survived that one. I overcame that one. Yeah, sure I made a bad decision then, but God, I was 12 years old or 18 years old or 22 years old or whatever. Look I still overcame it.' All of a sudden you start thinking man, that negative is really a positive."

Gene Landrum is a high-tech, start-up executive turned educator and writer. As a businessman he originated what we've all heard of—the Chuck E. Cheese concept of family entertainment—among other entrepreneurial ventures. After many years of interacting with creative and overachieving personalities, he began writing books about what makes the great people tick and this is where I've become a big fan. His doctoral work, *The Innovator Personality*, led to many books on the mental and emotional side of success. He also wrote *The Superman Syndrome: You Become What You Believe*.

"As you know I've spoken extensively about Henry Ford, who went to the fifth grade. He was in Detroit. Do you think he knew what he was doing? No, he actually got himself into some big trouble because the CPA, actually, chief financial officer, quit and brought a class action lawsuit against the guy in 1914 because he priced the Model T below what his cost was and that was a gut thing.

"What we're talking about here, Joe, is that very thing. Sometimes we know too much for our own good. We know so much, and you've heard me say this, Joe, on some of our interviews. I didn't know enough to know I couldn't have a rat delivering a pizza in a restaurant called Chuck E. Cheese and people were saying, "You're nuts man. We kill rats, you can't have a rat." I tell people I didn't know enough to know what I couldn't do so I did something that happened to turn out really quite good.

"When I was doing the research on Oprah, Oprah Winfrey, she was petrified when she was trying to . . . she was 20 years old . . . to go on her first network show and she says, "I don't know how to do that," and she sat. And a lot of your listeners may be thinking about this, 'Oh, how do I go in there and do this? How do I deal this and cut this new deal?'

"Well she looked and she thought about it, she's very bright, and she said, 'I know, today I'm not Oprah.' And I say this and I talked about this, as you know, in my *Superman* book a good bit. We almost have to con ourselves and almost go into a mythical fantasy role model, if you will, where you get beyond these fears and not be me. What Oprah did, she said, 'I know tonight I'm not Oprah, I'm Barbara,' because years ago Barbara Walters was the number one talk show host, and you know what she did. This is a true story, Joe.

"Your listeners get a handle on this. She actually dressed like Barbara dressed—she was from Tennessee, Barbara's from New York City. She dressed like Barbara. She taught herself to walk like Barbara, and walked out on that stage and acted like Barbara and she tried to talk like Barbara. You know what I find, Joe, so interesting about this motivationally? You know what—she's worth more than Barbara now. She's worth 2 billion dollars."

Arnold Patent has written numerous books, including *So, You Can Have It All*, which is still out there. Patent has also written *The Journey, Money, The Treasure Hunt*, and *Bridges to Reality*.

"That's why I wrote the book *The Journey*, to explain how is it that our lives are essentially opposite to our natural state. The principles defining, or describing, our natural state and yet we find ourselves experiencing virtually the opposite. And what I was guided to around that, to the coaching that I went through, was when I came up with describing as phase one and phase two.

"Phase one being the intentional creation of experiences opposite to our natural state. So, before we come into this incarnation, we plan out what family we're going to come into, what the belief systems, existence, are and so on. So, it's played out so in order to come into the human experience, we have to give up being who we really are, the power and presence of God, and any memory of that.

"See, we come from the oneness and our whole time in eternity is moving back into the oneness, but along the way, we explore other ways of experiencing ourselves and the human experience. This realm we're in is a very dense realm and one that we can only experience by making our lives opposite to their natural state. Then, like those people listening to this program and others, at a particular point, something occurs within you that says, 'Wait, there's more to life than what I've been experiencing up until now,' and that's where the seeking that you did, that I did, where we all did, searching for what's really going on. That's when we start the phase two part, the conscious movement back to our natural state.

"So, what's important about this is recognizing that essentially, each of us is the creator of the phase-one experience. We set out to make our lives opposite to our natural state and being the creator, we can also be the un-creator. I would add one other element to it.

"See, when we talk about creation, there's two levels of power. True power rests with the Divine. We cannot create at that level. We create with a small *c,* essentially, those creations are made up in our imagination. They're not real and they don't last in the sense, but we can make ourselves believe they're real, which we do, and so that's our human experience.

"Always illusory in a sense, always made up, but because of our creative power to create illusions, we can also create the belief that they're real. When you go into the awakening process, you start to segregate out the difference between our level of creation as human and creation at the Divine level."

THE SEVEN BLOCKS

W hen I was conducting my Rolls-Royce Phantom Masterminds, I met already successful people who knew they wanted more—more money, more success, more insight, more spirituality, more of the full life experience.

Many were millionaires or multimillionaires. Quite a few had widespread recognition, but only in relatively narrow niches. In short, most of these people were already highly successful by anyone's standards. But many wanted *worldwide* success. They were truly ready for the major leagues—they wanted to play the bigger game and make more of a difference for more people, in a much bigger way.

You could say that they wanted to become household names.

I loved helping these wonderful people attain widespread fame and new levels of financial success. Some were surprised, but I never was. I knew in advance what was possible for each person. Even so, I learned something new as I helped so many of them move to their own personal next levels.

Here is what I found: There was a surefire way to predict whether or not they would get where they said they wanted to go. It all boiled down to seven major blocks to worldwide success. Take a look at these and see how many of them could be holding *you* back from reaching *your* next level. In no particular order, here they are.

Your Dream Just Isn't Big Enough

It's gotta be BIG. *OUTRAGEOUSLY* BIG. Because if you don't have a clear, powerful enough vision—one that really excites you a lot and even scares you a little—then you just aren't going to do what it takes to get where you want to go. You see, to achieve worldwide fame, you need a big, bold dream to propel you into living that dream.

You need a vision to turn on the radar in your mind to seek and find opportunities and connections. Without a big dream—a goal, a desire, a vision—you will survive but not thrive; you will exist but not exhilarate.

How this worked in my own life: When I decided to become a musician at age 57, it was a scary yet exciting dream. But it was my big dream—that humongous vision—that gave me the energy and confidence to create 15 albums in less than five years. That made me more than enough money to buy some of the most expensive guitars in the world.

And most important of all: It was my humongous vision, ultimately, that got my music in the hands (and ears) of more people around the world than even *I* dreamed of!

You're Not Taking Consistent Action

Willingness to take action, and keep taking action, is a major factor. You don't need an entire step-by-step plan, as you might have to create it as you go. But you *do* need to take action.

Any action, even a baby step, is moving in the right direction. Because you have to keep moving forward for the path to unfold. The rest of the road will become clear as you do. It's like driving your car at night. You can only see the road as far as your headlights shine, but you can make the whole trip if you keep driving.

Personal example: Whenever I write a new book, I begin with the same blank page. But by typing words on it, I end up building what becomes a book. Many of them are worldwide bestsellers, such as *Zero Limits* and *The Key*.

You Aren't Congruent Enough in Your Beliefs

People who obtain worldwide success have an unreasonably strong—even stubborn—belief in themselves. If you don't believe in yourself, or in your dream, you probably won't take any action, or last very long. Limiting beliefs about money, success, yourself, and more, could limit your vision and curb your enthusiasm.

Your beliefs create your reality. Supportive beliefs can attract the massive success you want. Again, my decision to become a musician is relevant. I had no prior experience in singing, writing songs, recording them, or much else. As I systematically erased the limiting beliefs, using what I teach in my Miracles Coaching® program, I freed myself to pursue my dream.

You Lack the Necessary Courage

"No guts, no glory." It's true! It takes courage to face your fears, come from faith, and make a massive worldwide impact. You don't have to be flamboyant or showy, but you do have to be willing to step into the limelight. This is more about being willing to gamble on your dream than it is about being an extrovert. You can be shy and successful. But you have to have the inner faith in yourself to pursue your dream.

I've often said that whenever you go for a dream bigger than what you've attempted before, you will feel fear. It's natural. You are leaving your comfort zone. But as you take a deep breath and just do it, you find the inner power to get going, and the movement forward creates a momentum that is virtually unstoppable.

You're Not Willing to Do the Marketing

"Build it and they will come" works great in fictional stories, but face it: Nothing gets noticed unless somebody is marketing it (including the movie where the phrase "Build it and they will come" comes from!). The visionaries who are making a long-term difference on a worldwide scale all either conducted noteworthy marketing, or hired someone to do it.

Take Freud. While his ideas and books were being published and considered, they weren't reaching a wide audience. It took a marketer to do that. Edward L. Bernays, the father of modern public relations, was the nephew of Freud. He saw his uncle struggle and did something about it. Today, largely thanks to the marketing work of Bernays, Freud is a worldwide name.

You Didn't Launch the Skyrockets

Getting worldwide success means standing out in the crowd. Doing big things in a big way is how you send a skyrocket into the world and get people to turn your way.

Consider Trump. Love him or hate him, vote for him or not, he is getting his name and brand increasingly recognized around the world.

The same goes for Branson. His daredevil exploits and well-promoted adventures, from ballooning to space flights, get his name locked into the mind of the world.

You Haven't Vastly Exceeded Expectations

Ultimately, you need to surprise people with what you deliver. Your product or service has to be *way* more than promised or expected. It needs to wow them.

Zappos is known for this. So are many other companies that have worldwide recognition. They go beyond what is expected to deliver a wow service experience. Barnum, in the 1800s, did the same by offering tens of thousands of oddities in his museum. We still know his name today.

So, that is my list of the seven major blocks to worldwide success. Any one of them can stop you. All of them would have kept you from even reading this chapter. Now that you know them, the next step is yours.

BUTTERFLIES AND YOUR RAS

How many butterflies do you see around you? Right now, in your home or office, probably none. But you will probably notice a few later today—maybe in a magazine photo, or on television, or out in nature—at least until my question evaporates from your consciousness. Why?

In researching goal setting for a talk for the Texas Association of Magicians (TAOM) convention in Austin, Texas, I was reminded of our RAS. RAS means Reticular Activating System. It's at the base of your brain stem. Its job is to basically sort through the millions of data bits surrounding you in any one moment to deliver the seven bits that are relevant to you.

Numerous authors gave their own names to this natural tool of survival and selection. In 1960, Maxwell Maltz wrote a breakthrough book called *Psycho-Cybernetics*. In it he called the RAS your "servo-mechanism." Seems like an odd name to me, but it worked for Maltz and legions of his readers.

Either way, there is something in you that will help you attract your intentions if you activate it. So let's look a little closer. . . .

How Does Your RAS Select What's Relevant?

Basically in two ways:

1. Anything to help you survive.
2. Anything related to a goal.

Survival is the default setting. Your brain is designed to help you stay safe and reproduce. You don't have to think about it. It's hardwired into your brain.

Most of the work of your unconscious is around the idea of keeping you here and assuring some aspect of you remains after you're gone. But you can also program your mind for additional filters. For example, whenever you set a goal or intention, you are programming your mind to help you attract and achieve it.

You are inserting a new command into your RAS. It will then begin to filter those 10,000,000 bits of data in every moment to deliver what is relevant to your goal or intention. But how do you program your RAS?

The best way to get a new command into your brain is with a goal or intention that fulfills these three qualities:

1. Emotional
2. Vivid imagery
3. Repeated

In other words, a goal needs to be fueled with emotion (love, hate, or fear are the biggies); it needs to be vividly clear as an image (the mind responds to pictures); and it needs to be repeated (to get it installed in your mind).

When I asked you to look for butterflies, I was temporarily turning on your RAS to look for butterflies. Without an emotional reason to see butterflies, or a clear picture of what butterfly you wanted to see, and without repetition, you will soon forget all about butterflies. This is true for anything you want to attract or achieve.

Your mind is designed to help you achieve your goals, but you have to tell it what you want. Why not do that right now? Here's how:

1. Select a desire, goal, or intention.
2. Find an emotional reason for wanting it.
3. Create or find a clear image of it.
4. Look at the image, and feel your desire for it, every day.

Of course, you still need to take action.

Wallace Wattles (of *The Science of Getting Rich* fame) said what you want will arrive through *natural means*. Don't expect a Hollywood movie-style, Harry Potter production of your goal, but do welcome it if it comes that way.

Expect miracles—and do what you are inspired to do. Meanwhile, enjoy the butterflies.

HELP PARIS: THE POWER OF GROUP INTENT

As I type these words in late 2015, people in Paris have been traumatized by the surprise attacks on them, and are worried about family, friends, and their future well-being. While the world is still reeling from the effects of war, many are now bracing for something that could be worse.

As I overhear all of this, I hear an underlying victim mentality:

We're victims of storms.
We're victims of attacks.
We're victims of a poorly run government.
We're victims of gas prices, gas shortages, inflation, recession, taxes, wars, and more.

I'm going to say something unusual that may upset some people. I'm hoping it will inspire you. Here goes: You have more power than you think.

While you may not want to stand in the path of war, you don't have to cower under the bed. As odd as it may sound, I believe that if enough of us think positively, we can create a counter storm of sorts. We can protect ourselves and our loved ones with our thoughts.

I've described and proved this with the research in the back of my book *The Attractor Factor*. More than 19 studies proved that when a large group of people hold positive intentions, those intentions radiate out and become reality. I asked my readers to help stop Hurricane Rita almost 10 years ago. Rita stopped. I asked my readers to help stop the Texas wildfires several years ago. The fires stopped. I asked my readers to help my dying mother several years ago. My mother is still with us. Together, we can do something about Paris, too.

I'm not saying ignore current reality. I'm asking you to create a better reality. I'm saying don't get caught up in fear. I'm asking you to come from faith. If you think an attack will get you or a loved one, then it's already gotten you: you're living in fear. Your life is dark, gloomy, and in a cage.

The media is flawless at whipping us into fear, so I suggest ignoring the mainstream media. It's not information; it's propaganda. That's why it's called programming. It gets large groups of people to think negatively, which of course then becomes reality. Why can't we do the opposite?

Why can't we get large groups of people to think positive? Yes, be sure to travel safely and wisely. Yes, be sure you take care of yourself and your family. Yes, contribute to any causes you believe in that help people who need it right now. But also check the storehouse in your mind:

Are you living in fear, or living in trust?

Are you coming from fear, or faith?

Are you focused on the negative, or are you doing something to create a positive?

We are always at choice.

My plea is that the readers of this manifesto—you—will stop, breathe, and focus on love; pray, or in some positive way send out an energy that will help dissolve the fear in and around us. I'm asking you to do this today.

As I was writing this, I was reminded of the famous *Paradoxical Commandments* written by Dr. Kent M. Keith.

> *People are illogical, unreasonable, and self-centered.*
> > *Love them anyway.*
> *If you do good, people will accuse you of selfish ulterior motives.*
> > *Do good anyway.*
> *If you are successful, you will win false friends and true enemies.*
> > *Succeed anyway.*
> *The good you do today will be forgotten tomorrow.*
> > *Do good anyway.*
> *Honesty and frankness make you vulnerable.*
> > *Be honest and frank anyway.*

The biggest men and women with the biggest ideas can be shot down by
the smallest men and women with the smallest minds.
Think big anyway.
People favor underdogs but follow only top dogs.
Fight for a few underdogs anyway.
What you spend years building may be destroyed overnight.
Build anyway.
People really need help but may attack you if you do help them.
Help people anyway.
Give the world the best you have and you'll get kicked in the teeth.
Give the world the best you have anyway.

I know you may feel that thinking positively may be a waste of time.
Do it anyway.
I know you may feel that your efforts are insignificant.
Do it anyway.
I know you may wonder if group meditation will really work.
Do it anyway.
I know you may doubt if prayer will help.
Do it anyway.
Let's create the positive future we want right now. Let's focus on spirit. Let's focus on love. What I'm asking you to do is be happy, right now.

Smile.

Send that loving energy out, in the direction of Paris. Intend for all to be well, for, in reality, from a spiritual view of life, all is well. We can make a difference. It begins with you and me.

Will you join me?

THE FOURTH-DIMENSION PROCESS: TRIGGERING HYPERMANIFESTATION FOR WEALTH

An attempt at visualizing the Fourth Dimension: Take a point, stretch it into a line, curl it into a circle, twist it into a sphere, and punch through that sphere.

—Einstein

Perception has a destiny.

—Emerson

I'm shaking as I write this. This special report is my first explanation of the fourth-dimension process. I'm excited. It works. I believe it holds the key to a new world of possibilities because, in the fourth dimension, anything really is possible!

Let me explain—and prove—it to you: Most people are trying to manifest what they want by working within an unconscious set of limiting beliefs. They don't know it, but their current reality was created by their existing unconscious mindset. Until they change their paradigm, it will be difficult to create any lasting, dramatic new change, whether to increase wealth or anything else. They will just keep playing in the same sandbox.

This illustration helps explain the issue:

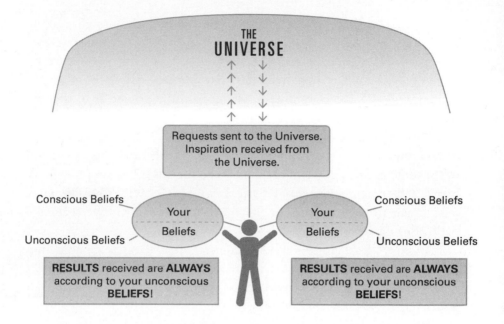

The image shows that the filter sorting through everything—from inspirations to intentions—is in the unconscious mind. That filter is our belief system. Whether anyone allows something into their life—wealth, romance, or anything else—depends on what is in their unconscious mind.

If they have beliefs about, for example, money being bad or evil, then that belief will prevent money from coming in or staying. Being considered bad, the person will get rid of money fast—but rarely know why. They will blame their lack on others and virtually never look in the mirror. It will rarely if ever occur to them that their beliefs are creating their results.

To help resolve this issue, I created a method to break free. I call it the fourth-dimension process, which is a nod toward where we have to go to create a new reality: outside of our current reality.

Outside to where? To what some call the fourth dimension. To explain this process, let's begin with a straight line:

That line is a symbol for a flat dimension, what some might call the first dimension. When people write affirmations, they are trying to create change within one dimension—a very limited and not very powerful one. You can make change from this view, but not easily, or quickly, or everlastingly. It's too one-dimensional. It has little power. It is, after all, just a line.

Another step up is to visualize what you want. This adds depth to the desire, which makes it more two-dimensional, at least in the perception of the mind. Some people use a vision board for this. They simply create a board with images representing what they want to have, do, or be. They post it where they will see it the most, usually the refrigerator or a bathroom mirror.

A vision board is a tool to communicate desires to the subconscious mind. While some boards have multiple desires represented on them, a more powerful approach would be to take one desire—to have singular focus—and use a meaningful image to represent it.

For example, I want a vintage 1955 Mercedes Sl300 Gullwing, generally considered the world's first supercar. I would take an image of the car and put it where I could see it. Looking at the image of the real car and visualizing it is a more two-dimensional approach to creating, attracting, or manifesting. Imagery is powerful and has been proven to work, in everything from sports to medicine to business. But you are still working within a limited dimension, and still working within existing limiting beliefs. You can imagine wealth all you like, but if you still believe it's bad for you, you won't see opportunities to obtain it. While you can achieve great results with imagery, it has built-in limitations. It is still a boxed in way to live, let alone try to transform.

Yet another level up is to imagine already owning the car, driving the car, sharing the car with friends—bringing yourself into involvement with the image itself. This is entering a more third-dimensional experience of manifestation. Instead of writing an affirmation (first dimension) or seeing the car separate from you (second dimension) you move into an almost holographic experience of already enjoying the car in present time, as if it is real right now. This is moving near the third dimension—the physical reality we all share as humans—and making the desire as concrete as possible. This is better, but not best. Obviously, all three approaches work, but with limitations.

- Writing affirmations is flat and one-dimensional, so it has little (but not no) ability to create change. You'll have to do a lot of writing and affirming to overwrite the existing programs in your mind.
- Visualizing what you want, whether a new car or great wealth, is a step into the second dimension because it brings what you want to life in your mind. This approach gives your desire more shape, color, depth, and emotion, which are all-important to the second dimension. But, you are still limited by what you believe is possible.
- The third dimension interactive visualization is much like your day-to-day experience: it feels real. So imagining that what you want is already done, and so real that it might pass for reality, will speed up your results. Again, even this dimension is still working within what you currently (but probably unknowingly) believe.

How can you leave all limitations, all limiting beliefs, and all boxed mindsets, and enter a world where you know anything is possible and can manifest from that place of all possibilities?

Enter the fourth dimension.

I started to entertain the idea of a fourth dimension to reality almost a decade ago, after reading a 1949 book by Neville Goddard, *Out of this World*. He has a chapter in it called "Thinking Fourth-Dimensionally." Here's an excerpt:

> *Here is a technique that makes it easy to encounter events before they occur, to "call things which are not seen as though they were" [Romans 4:17]. People have a habit of slighting the importance of simple things; but this simple formula for changing the future was discovered after years of searching and experimenting.*
>
> *The first step in changing the future is desire—that is: define your objective—know definitely what you want.*
>
> *Secondly: construct an event which you believe you would encounter following the fulfillment of your desire—an event which implies fulfillment of your desire—something that will have the action of self predominant.*
>
> *Thirdly: immobilize the physical body and induce a condition akin to sleep—lie on a bed or relax in a chair and imagine that you are sleepy; then, with eyelids closed and your attention focused on the action you intend to experience—in imagination—mentally feel yourself right into*

the proposed action—imagining all the while that you are actually performing the action here and now. You must always participate in the imaginary action, not merely stand back and look on, but you must feel that you are actually performing the action so that the imaginary sensation is real to you.

It is important always to remember that the proposed action must be one that follows the fulfillment of your desire; and, also, you must feel yourself into the action until it has all the vividness and distinctness of reality.

For example: suppose you desired promotion in office. Being congratulated would be an event you would encounter following the fulfillment of your desire. Having selected this action as the one you will experience in imagination, immobilize the physical body, and induce a state akin to sleep—a drowsy state—but one in which you are still able to control the direction of your thoughts—a state in which you are attentive without effort. Now, imagine that a friend is standing before you. Put your imaginary hand into his. First feel it to be solid and real, and then carry on an imaginary conversation with him in harmony with the action. Do not visualize yourself at a distance in point of space and at a distance in point of time being congratulated on your good fortune. Instead, make elsewhere here, and the future now. The future event is a reality now in a dimensionally larger world; and, oddly enough, now in a dimensionally larger world, is equivalent to here in the ordinary three-dimensional space of everyday life.

The difference between feeling yourself in action, here and now, and visualizing yourself in action, as though you were on a motion-picture screen, is the difference between success and failure.

The difference will be appreciated if you will now visualize yourself climbing a ladder. Then with eyelids closed imagine that a ladder is right in front of you and feel you are actually climbing it.

Neville was explaining a way for us to create a third-dimensional reality (the one we live in) out of a fourth-dimensional experience (the one ideas come from). He was on the right track, but he couldn't articulate or elaborate on the process with enough clarity to help most people. He also wasn't a hypnotist, or a coach. He was a mystic.

He also wasn't the first to talk about a fourth dimension. In 1916, Claude Bragdon wrote a book called, *Four-Dimensional Vistas.* In the

1925 edition that I have, he attempts to describe this new dimension this way: "Our space cannot contain it, because it contains no space. No walls separate us from this demesne, not even the walls of our fleshly prison; yet we may not enter, even though we are already 'there.' It is the place of dreams, of living dead men; it is At the Back of the North Wind and Behind the Looking Glass."

Besides Bragdon's pioneering book, there are numerous works in mathematics and theoretical physics that describe a fourth dimension. And let's not forget the sci-fi writers. There's Rod Serling and his fifth dimension, which he called *The Twilight Zone*, which was usually more frightening than enlightening. It made for good television. But it also pointed to another world within this one.

What I've done is take the seed of an idea, which Neville offered in 1949, and transformed it into the Wealth Transformation Process.

Now let me describe how this process works, using the 1955 Gullwing as an example:

A one-dimensional approach would be to write an affirmation, such as, "I now own that 1955 Mercedes SL300 Gullwing (or something better)." (I always use the disclaimer phrase, "This or something better," to allow for the possibility of a better result than what my mind can currently imagine.) I'd have to write that line 500 times a day, every day, for who knows how long, for it to make a dent in my unconscious. It's too flat as a method of rapid manifestation.

A two-dimensional approach would be to visualize the car. I would at least be adding depth and length to the desire, which helps bring it to life, at least mentally. Since the subconscious responds to imagery, this is a step in the right direction. But I might look at the image every day for months to years and never attract the actual car. It's not enough.

A third-dimensional approach would be to imagine myself driving the car, owning the car, parking the car, holding the keys to the car, taking photos of the car, and so forth. Because this actively adds me into the imagery, it would get the request into my deeper mind faster. This is good.

But a fourth-dimensional approach would be to imagine I live in a world with no limits, no beliefs, no restraints—where anything is possible because it holds the vastness of time and space. This open realm of all possibilities is where I would go by inducing a trance—or having a hypnotist or coach guide me there—and pretending I am now in the dream world that precedes this concrete world. I am in the White Board (to use a term from my books, such as *Zero Limits*) of all beginnings.

In this fourth dimension, I would simply allow the car into my life. There would be no wanting, desiring, longing; it would be mine by the very nature of anything goes in this other dimension. I would simply allow it, accept it, and welcome it. No addiction. No attachment. No need. No stress.

While this last step might seem far out or esoteric, there are enough mystery schools and metaphysical studies to state that this is where all life begins.

Obviously, adding Miracles Coaching®, hypnosis, recorded guided audio inductions, or The Remembering Process, would be great tools to make this fourth dimension more accessible. After all, people can still enter their version of the fourth dimension and still have limits/beliefs/blocks preventing them from creating in an open-ended way. They may still be seeing reality through the filter of their unconscious beliefs. This is why I believe having a Miracles Coach, or working with a trained hypnotist, will still be needed by most people. (Note: Mathew Dixon and I created Fourth Dimension Music to accompany whatever hypnosis/coaching/remembering anyone might add to enter the Fourth Dimension. See www.TheFourthDimensionMusic.com.)

Does this process work? Brace yourself. Here's what happened one day later (!) from my doing this fourth-dimension process on that original 1955 Mercedes Gullwing:

First, I felt I should find out what the vintage car for sale actually cost. No price was listed on the site. I called, spoke to the owner, and was told this particular pristine, collectible car could go for only $1,950,000. I thanked him. I hung up. I wasn't discouraged, as all I was doing was seeking information. I just filed it in my mind and thought, "I wonder where the money will come from?" and "This car or something better."

Second, the next morning I felt inspired to check eBay for any listings of Gullwing cars. There were several toy model cars for sale, and I bid on one. I figured having a small scale version of the actual car would help me experience the car in a more third-dimension way: it'd have shape and contours and lines, and so on. I'd be able to hold it and imagine the real thing.

While I was still at eBay, I noticed a Gullwing for sale. It surprised me. Mercedes has made modern Gullwing cars over the years, and I drove one years ago, but didn't like the bulk or power of it. But this listing was for a replica car, built in 2007. The car looked exactly like a 1955 Mercedes 300SL Gullwing but was actually hand built, using a Chevy motor and transmission, to duplicate one.

This appealed to me instantly, mainly because the original car didn't have air conditioning, and this replicated version did. (There's interesting footage online of people driving original Gullwing cars down the road with the Gullwing doors swung high and open, trying to get some air.) And there's the added value of having a newer car, with parts that any GM dealer could work on or replace.

I immediately saw this listing as a "This or something better" opportunity. I wrote to the seller and asked information about the car. He quickly replied, and his answers made me even more excited. I decided to bid on the car.

I got slightly worried that the auction would get out of hand, as auctions often do, and the bidding would skyrocket, right past what the car was actually worth. But then I remembered that in the fourth dimension, there are no limits of time or space. I would just own the car and forget about how it came to me. So I let my worry go.

And then the seller contacted me again. He already had numerous offers (more than 100, from all over the world) for the car, but said if I met a little less than his reserve price, he'd end the auction and sell the car to me right now. He wouldn't have to wait days for his money or wonder what the car would sell for or where it would go. He'd be done and I'd have the car. Win–win.

The car, new, sold for $180,000. Only a dozen had been made. It was still pristine, ran perfectly, and only had 650 miles on it. In my mind I had already decided I wanted it but would not pay more than $100k for it. The seller wanted $89k. I offered $80k. He accepted.

The car is being shipped to me right now. I will own it in a week— after using the fourth-dimension process barely 24 hours ago!

This all happened so fast, and so easily and effortlessly, that I'm still shaken (in a joyous way) and still processing the experience.

And remember: I wanted the car for almost a decade, had it on a vision board for almost two years, dreamed about it and talked about it, but didn't actually attract it until the next day after doing the fourth-dimension process only once. (!)

As I wrote in the beginning, this special report is my first explanation of the fourth dimension process. I'm excited because it works. Again, I believe it holds the magic key to a new world of miraculous possibilities for people because—in the fourth dimension—anything really is possible!

My Gullwing is proof. The only problem is, now I need to manifest another parking place.

INSIDE THE CREED

Throughout the manifesto, you found the core tenants of the Awakened Millionaire: "The Awakened Millionaire's Creed."

At the heart of everything you do as an Awakened Millionaire is the creed. Every action you take, every intuitive direction you follow, every intention you set, and every decision you make lies the creed. Your passion, your purpose, and your mission are in direct alignment with the creed. It is the bedrock of your entire journey. And while you will be a unique expression of the Awakened Millionaire, we all use this creed to guide us and unite us.

So it's important you understand what each element of the creed is, what it stands for, and how to translate it into reality.

Let's begin.

Awakened Millionaires Are Driven First by Their Passion, Purpose, and Mission

There is no Awakened Millionaire without passion, purpose, and mission. It is, and will always be, your source of direction, strength, and light. If you anchor yourself deeply within your passion, purpose, and mission, you will never stray far from your path. It is due north for your internal compass.

As you traveled with me through this manifesto, you experienced exciting aspects and opportunities waiting for you. Perhaps it's the thrill of a transformed relationship with money. Perhaps it's activating the fundamental power of your intuition. Perhaps it's the idea of money and soul working together in harmony to lift you and your mission to the level of resonance it's capable of becoming.

But unless you are crystal clear on your mission, guided by your passion, and anchored in your purpose, you will be wandering aimlessly through this adventure. This is not an option.

Your passion is the resonance of your soul, the immense pull that guides your heart, and the candy for your imagination. Where you find your greatest loves in life is where you find your passion. Where you would spend all your time and money if you had no barriers is where you find your passion. Find your passion and don't let go.

Your purpose is the articulation of your passion into the real world. This is how you put your passion into action. How do you find your purpose? You listen deeply to your soul's calling. You cannot force it. You cannot sculpt it with your intellect. You must find the internal point of pure resonance that speaks to you. And until you find this purpose, this expression of your passion, you do not move forward. Instead, you turn inward, you open up your soul's ears and listen for the voice that points you where you must go. You will find it if it's not already obvious. Remain patient and vigilant, as we all have purpose swelling within us. We simply must remain open.

Combine your passion and purpose, and you have your mission as an Awakened Millionaire. This becomes your unshakable foundation. Life throws many twists and turns at you. But you have spread your roots with your mission, and you will be able to bend with the wind without losing your grounding. Perhaps your mission is evident in everything you do. Perhaps it's simply an understanding that only you need to know. But whatever it is, it can be seen in everything you do.

Find your passion. Find your purpose. Find your mission. This is the way of the Awakened Millionaire.

The Awakened Millionaire Uses Money as a Soulful Tool to Make a Positive Impact

The Awakened Millionaire walks with a transformed relationship with money. There is no gray area here. There are no doubts about the neutral nature of money. The thought of money holding any control of you is distant. It is the old you.

Money is now at your disposal to express your mission and direct the intentions of your soul. You fill it with your calling, with your soulful purpose, and let it support your mission. You always use it as a tool for creating an impact in this world. It is only through this evolved relationship with money that you can become the Awakened Millionaire that makes a difference in the world around you.

There is nothing wrong with enjoying the luxuries that money offers you. This is not a call to give all your money away. This is not a call to live an ascetic's lifestyle. Enjoy the benefits of money. Enjoy the tastes of luxury. Treat yourself to the rewards that money can bring you.

But never lose sight in the ultimate purpose of money: to help translate your mission into an impact the world will feel for generations to come.

The Awakened Millionaire Is Persistently Empowered, Believing in Themselves Absolutely

You are a shining example of power to all those who encounter you. In a world suffering from the mentality of victimhood, you have transcended these old bonds and attained true empowerment. You have claimed responsibility for your life, in all aspects. You understand that the fundamental nature of empowerment does not come from trying to control everything that happens to you. You understand that empowerment comes from taking responsibility for how you respond to every situation you encounter, every challenge you face, and every roadblock that might stand in front of you.

Carry this torch of empowerment, and you will naturally believe in yourself. They go hand in hand. You cannot be empowered without believing in yourself, as with the empowerment comes a simple understanding: no matter what you face, you are ready, willing, and very capable of handling anything and everything, no matter how challenging or monumental.

The Awakened Millionaire Is Committed to Grow, Improve, Reinvent, and Always Discover

You understand implicitly that there is no stagnation found in the life of an Awakened Millionaire. Becoming an Awakened Millionaire is not an unmoving point you reach. Becoming an Awakened Millionaire is a space, a mindset, and a flow that is constantly shifting with the whims of life. If you stand still and refuse change, you will return to a stagnant lifestyle, and your mission will suffer.

That's why you are always, now and forever, committed to growth. You are committed to pushing yourself to learn new skills, improve your gifts, reinvent yourself as a perpetually evolving soul, and discover the hidden treasures of life you only find when you embrace the spirit of adventure. You are never stagnant. You are always growing.

The Awakened Millionaire Is Unshakably Bold, Takes Risks, and Does Not Hesitate

While others cower at the thought of risk and bold action, you embrace it with every aspect of your being. While others feel fear, you feel joy and adventure. You are bold. You are always bold. You thrive on bold action.

You take risks because you understand it is the only way to uncover new opportunity. You take risks because you understand that what others call failure is actually simple feedback and opportunity for growth. You feel no fear in the thought of failure. You embrace it. You embody this fearlessness.

As a result, you never hesitate. You may slow down to consider your options, but you never hesitate out of fear. You are fearless. You are bold. You understand there is only reward found in decisive action, because failure is no longer a reality. There is only growth.

The Awakened Millionaire Is Guided by the Soulful Resonance of Their Intuition

While others battle with indecision, you smoothly flow through your adventure, step by step. While others experience the paralysis of over-analysis, you are equipped with the Awakened Millionaire's secret weapon: your intuition.

The intuition is a direct conduit to your soulful purpose. It is an expression of your divine nature. It understands what to do faster and more thoroughly than your conscious, logical mind could ever fathom. It is the bedrock of your decision-making.

While others marvel at your ability to choose the best path for your journey, you understand that you are actually taking the easy road. You are simply trusting your intuition, for your intuition will always lead you wherever you must go, even if your conscious mind cannot understand the reasons why. You have complete faith in your intuition, so you never falter.

The Awakened Millionaire Knows Wealth Is Everything They Have, Not Just Money

You, as the Awakened Millionaire, are the embodiment of wealth. You understand that wealth is everything you have, not just your money. If you lose all your money, you will still be wealthy. In this understanding of wealth, you find the full arsenal of tools at your disposal. Yes, money can give you great power to make an impact. It can be a mighty and soulful tool to actualize your mission. But it is only one tool among many.

Your wealth is made up of your skills, your talents, your passion, your purpose, your mission, your flexibility, your resources, your circles, your support, and your personal power.

And as you elevate yourself as an Awakened Millionaire, you always elevate your wealth at the same time.

The Awakened Millionaire Holds a Deep Gratitude for All They Have and Achieve

The Awakened Millionaire takes nothing for granted. You understand that every aspect of your life, your success, and your path is a gift, and you radiate that gratitude in everything you do. Gratitude is not only the evolved way of living—it is a powerful tool in the hands of the Awakened Millionaire. Others gravitate towards the expression of gratitude. It is a magnet for people who will support you, help elevate you, and ultimately move you forward.

The gratitude always travels to your core. It is your constant companion. Life is precious. Your wealth is precious. Your mission is precious—and you never forget this.

The Awakened Millionaire Is Permanently Connected to Universal Abundance

The Awakened Millionaire never thinks there's not enough. You see that all around you, every day, are opportunities to bring prosperous abundance into your life. The amount of money in circulation is in the trillions at any moment. There is never a shortage.

You become a master of tapping into this universal abundance. Where you go, abundance follows. You are not full of tricks to create abundance. You do not seek shortcuts or quick fixes. You are simply in touch, permanently connected to the overwhelming abundance waiting for all of us.

The Awakened Millionaire Is Generous, Ethical, and Focuses on the Good of Others

The Awakened Millionaire is never selfish, self-centered, or greedy. All of your personal and entrepreneurial efforts are rooted in solid ethical principles and are always focused on the good of others. You do not think about taking advantage of situations. You do not think about yourself over the well-being of others. Your generosity and spirit of giving is around you, emanating outward for all to see.

At the same time, you understand that this philosophy of action, rooted in the betterment of others, is in fact one of the secrets to abundance itself. While some are trapped in a cycle of greed and self-interest, they are blind to the fact that, while they may have short-term gains, they will never achieve the level of success and fulfillment available to those who are rooted in generosity and ethical action.

The Awakened Millionaire Champions the Win–Win–Win

The win–win relationship is a step up from a greed perspective on gain, but the Awakened Millionaire always strives to take it one step further. You champion the win–win–win relationship: you win, your partner or customer wins, and the world around you wins as a result.

The win–win–win relationship is an expression of understanding about the world's inherent interconnectedness. Every aspect of our actions ripples out and affects everything in our path. So we are not only responsible for the effect of our actions, but we understand that in this natural order there is opportunity to expand our impact and make a great difference.

The Awakened Millionaire always asks, "How many people can win by this decision? How can I multiply the impact I can make?"

The Awakened Millionaire Soulfully Shares Their Entrepreneurial Gifts

The Awakened Millionaire is the entrepreneur. It is how you transform your passion into profit, and your mission into soulful money. At the same time, the Awakened Millionaire infuses soulful purpose and mission in every entrepreneurial venture. Your business is an expression of your soul. Your products or services are an expression of your mission. There is no disconnect between who you are and what you offer to the customers you serve. There is no separation.

Your business is an extension of yourself. It is a representation of yourself. You always respect the power that you have as an entrepreneur and treat every business decision with the appropriate gravity.

The Awakened Millionaire Leads by Example as the Catalyst for Transformation in Others

No matter what your individual mission is, the transformation of others is a mission found in every Awakened Millionaire. You lead by example. You transform others by example. At the core of it is an understanding: the more people who follow the "Awakened Millionaire's Creed," the more people who are dedicated to making a difference, to elevating themselves and their relationship with money, and to championing the transcendence of all souls . . . the more we all benefit, the more we all transform, the more we all become shining beacons of a soulful existence.

You understand that we live in a world that's in trouble. Whether it's the suffering of others, injustice, poverty, sickness, or an environment on the brink of disaster, you know that we need all hands on deck. You know that every person you bring to live through this creed is another person empowered and committed to helping all of us improve our station in life.

You do not preach, you do not proselytize. You lead by example. Others will watch you, learn, wonder, and be inspired.

YOUR NEXT STEP

You now have the foundation of the Awakened Millionaire at your fingertips. You now understand the opportunities that wait for you. You understand the power of the "Awakened Millionaire's Creed." You understand the new relationship with money waiting for you . . . and what that can mean for your impact. You understand how powerless you've been trapped in the victimhood mindset and how powerful you can become when taking responsibility for your every action. You understand how you are shaped by your passion, purpose, and mission. You understand how the Awakened Millionaire approaches entrepreneurship. You understand the fundamental path to transforming your passion into profit. But what's next?

How do you take the next step to transforming yourself into the Awakened Millionaire?

What is the next step to transform this manifesto into the new dawn you seek?

There is a practical way forward.

I created the Awakened Millionaire Academy to give you the exact steps you must take to make the ultimate transformation into the Awakened Millionaire. This advanced, step-by-step approach leaves nothing to question. It gives you the skills and knowledge you need. It gives you the next step. It shows you the eight laws to transform money into its ultimate soulful tool. It shows you the four steps to awakening. It shows you how to think, how to act, and what steps to take. It shows you how to realize your entrepreneurial dreams. It shows you the practical steps to transforming your passion into profit. It shows you everything you need to elevate, accelerate, and actualize your transformation and, as an owner of the manifesto, you get unprecedented access no one else gets.

It's waiting for you here:

wwww.awakenedmillionaireacademy.com/begin

Thank you for taking this journey with me. I hope you'll join me in the journey ahead. Together, we can transform the world.

Love,

Joe

P.S. I also invite you to check out Miracles Coaching® at www .MiraclesCoaching.com.

RESOURCES

Awakened Millionaire	www.awakenedmillionaireacademy.com
Dr. Joe Vitale	www.JoeVitale.com
Miracles Coaching®	www.MiraclesCoaching.com
Fourth Dimension Music	www.TheFourthDimensionMusic.com
Hypnotic Gold	www.HypnoticGold.com
Dr. Vitale Twitter:	https://twitter.com/mrfire
Dr. Vitale Facebook:	https://www.facebook.com/drjoevitale
Dr. Vitale Blog:	http://blog.mrfire.com/
Self-Help Music	www.allhealingmusic.com
Statbrook	http://statbrook.com/wp/
Paradoxical Commandments	www.paradoxicalcommandments.com/
Group Meditation	www.worldpeacegroup.org/world_peace_through_meditation.html
Secret Prayer	www.thesecretprayer.com

BIBLIOGRAPHY

Audlin, Mindy. *What If It All Goes Right?* New York: Morgan James, 2010.

Barton, Bruce. *The Man Nobody Knows.* New York: Bobbs-Merrill, 1925.

Barton, Bruce. *What Can a Man Believe?* New York: Bobbs-Merrill, 1927.

Bowen, Will. *A Complaint-Free World.* New York: Harmony, 2013.

Bragdon, Claude. *Four-Dimensional Vistas.* New York: Knopf, 1925.

Breuning, Loretta. *Beyond Cynical.* San Francisco: Inner Mammal Institute, 2013.

Bristol, Calude. *The Magic of Believing.* New York: Pocket Books, 1948.

Carnegie, Dale. *How to Win Friends and Influence People.* New York: Simon & Schuster, 1936.

Carr, Allen. *Packing It In.* New York: Penguin, 2005.

Dixon, Mathew. *Attracting for Others.* New Braunfels, TX: Zero Limits, 2012.

Ebeling, Mick. *Not Impossible.* New York, Atira Books, 2015.

Ford, Debbie. *The Dark Side of the Light Chasers.* New York: Penguin, 1999.

Fox, Emmet. *The Mental Equivalent.* Life Summit, MO: Unity, 1932.

Gage, Randy. *Risky Is the New Safe.* Hoboken, NJ: John Wiley & Sons, 2012.

Goddard, Neville. *Out of This World: Thinking Fourth-Dimensionally.* Eastford, CT: Martino Books, 2010.

Goddard, Neville. *Neville Goddard Lecture Series.* 12 volumes. Albuquerque, NM: Audio Enlightenment Press, 2014.

Goddard, Neville. *The Neville Reader.* Camarillo, CA: DeVorss, 2005.

Keith, Kent. *Anyway: The Paradoxical Commandments.* New York: Putnam, 2001.

Larson, Christian D. *Your Forces and How to Use Them.* London, UK: L.N. Fowler, 1912.

Patent, Arnold. *Money.* Kansas City, MO: Celebration Publishing, 2005.

Pilzer, Paul Zane. *The Next Millionaires.* New York: Momentum Media, 2006.

Landrum, Gene. *The Superman Syndrome.* Nashville, TN: iUniverse, 2005.

Lapin, Rabbi Daniel. *Thou Shall Prosper.* Hoboken, NJ: John Wiley & Sons, 2009.

Maltz, Maxwell. *Psycho-Cybernetics.* New York: Pocket Books, 1989.

McLaughlin, Corinne, and Gordon Davidson. *The Practical Visionary.* Minneapolis, MN: Unity, 2010.

Vitale, Joe. *The Awakening Course*. Hoboken, NJ: John Wiley, 2016.

Vitale, Joe. *Attract Money Now*. Austin, TX: Hypnotic Marketing, 2009.

Vitale, Joe. *The Attractor Factor*. Hoboken, NJ: John Wiley & Sons, 2006.

Vitale, Joe. *Life's Missing Instruction Manual*. Hoboken, NJ: John Wiley & Sons, 2006.

Vitale, Joe. *Miracles Manual*. 3 volumes. Free at www.miraclesmanual.com

Vitale, Joe. *There's a Customer Born Every Minute*. Hoboken, NJ: John Wiley & Sons, 2006.

Vitale, Joe, and Daniel Barrett. *The Remembering Process*. San Diego, CA: Hay House, 2014.

Vitale, Joe. *The Secret Prayer*. Austin, TX: CreateSpace, 2015.

Vitale, Joe. *The Secret to Attracting Money*. Audio course. Chicago: Nightingale–Conant, 2008.

Vitale, Joe. *The Seven Lost Secrets of Success*. Hoboken, NJ: John Wiley, 2007.

Vitale, Joe. *Zen and the Art of Writing*. San Diego: Westcliff Publications, 1984.

Wattles, Wallace. *Financial Success Through Creative Thought or The Science of Getting Rich*. Holyoke, MA: Elizabeth Towne, 1915.

Young, Vash. *A Fortune to Share*. New York: Bobbs-Merrill, 1931.

ABOUT THE AUTHOR

Dr. Joe Vitale—once homeless but now a motivating *inspirator* known to his millions of fans as "Mr. Fire!"—is the globally famous author of numerous bestselling books, such as *The Attractor Factor*, *Zero Limits*, *Life's Missing Instruction Manual*, *The Secret Prayer*, and *Attract Money Now* (free at www.AttractMoneyNow.com).

He is a star in the blockbuster movie *The Secret*, as well as a dozen other films. He has recorded many bestselling audio programs, from *The Missing Secret* to *The Zero Point*. He's also the world's first self-help singer-songwriter, with 15 albums out and many of his songs nominated for the Posi Award (considered the Grammys of positive music). He's also traveled the world as a rousing public speaker, visiting countries from Russia, Peru, and Kuwait to Poland, Bermuda, and Italy.

He created Miracles Coaching®, www.MiraclesCoaching.com, The Awakening Course, The Secret Mirror, Hypnotic Writing, and many more life-transforming products. He lives outside of Austin, Texas, with his wife, Nerissa, and their pets. His main website is www.JoeVitale.com.

Join the Awakened Millionaire Movement

www.awakenedmillionaireacademy.com/begin

Get a Free Miracles Coaching® consultation at www.MiraclesCoaching.com.

Follow Dr. Joe Vitale

Twitter: https://twitter.com/mrfire
Facebook: https://www.facebook.com/drjoevitale
Blog: http://blog.mrfire.com/

INDEX